Reverse Mortgages and Linked Securities

Founded in 1807, John Wiley & Sons is the oldest independent publishing company in the United States. With offices in North America, Europe, Australia and Asia, Wiley is globally committed to developing and marketing print and electronic products and services for our customers' professional and personal knowledge and understanding.

The Wiley Finance series contains books written specifically for finance and investment professionals as well as sophisticated individual investors and their financial advisors. Book topics range from portfolio management to e-commerce, risk management, financial engineering, valuation and financial instrument analysis, as well as much more.

For a list of available titles, please visit our Web site at www .WileyFinance.com.

Reverse Mortgages and Linked Securities

The Complete Guide to Risk, Pricing, and Regulation

VISHAAL BHUYAN

WILEY

John Wiley & Sons, Inc.

Published by John Wiley & Sons, Inc., Hoboken, New Jersey.

Published simultaneously in Canada.

For general information on our other products and services or for technical support, please contact our Customer Care Department within the United States at (800) 762-2974, outside the United States at (317) 572-3993 or fax (317) 572-4002.

Wiley also publishes its books in a variety of electronic formats. Some content that appears in print may not be available in electronic books. For more information about Wiley products, visit our web site at www.wiley.com.

Library of Congress Cataloging-in-Publication Data:
Bhuyan, Vishaal B., 1983-
    Reverse mortgages and linked securities : the complete guide to risk, pricing, and regulation / Vishaal Bhuyan.
        p. cm. — (Wiley finance series ; 577)
    Includes index.
    ISBN 978-0-470-58462-0 (hardback)
    1. Mortgage loans, Reverse—United States. I. Title.
    HG2040.15.B48 2011
    332.7'22—dc22

                                                                    2010023295

Printed in the United States of America

10 9 8 7 6 5 4 3 2 1

To FIFA
1999–2008

Contents

Preface

Over the past few years, seniors and soon-to-be retirees (Baby Boomers) have lost tremendous value in their retirement plans and especially in their home values. In addition to the depreciation of assets held by this group of Americans, unprecedented amounts of leverage used to finance their daily living, automobile purchases, and children's educations, as well as to purchase primary and even secondary residences in many cases, have left a large number of older Americans on the brink of financial ruin.

The *Baby Boomers* (born between 1946 and 1960) currently comprise 26 percent of the population of the United States or roughly 78 million people. Encompassing two cohorts (people born between 1946 and 1955 make up the first cohort and the second cohort, aka "Generation Jones," is made up of people born from 1956 to 1964), the Boomer generation is one of the largest and wealthiest demographics in U.S. history. According to a study conducted by McKinsey & Company, the wealth of the Baby Boomers can be attributed to three major factors:

1. Size
2. Social change
3. Education

Clearly, the sheer size of the Baby Boomers cohort allowed them to generate more income on a collective basis, being that this generation is some 50 percent larger than the previous generation. Baby Boomers have earned an estimated $2 trillion more (roughly $3.7 trillion) than the previous generation had at the same age. Moreover, the Baby Boomers were the first generation to experience a much higher number of female workers, which also meant women having children at a later age and staying in the workplace for longer periods of time. Finally, the Boomer generation was one of the most educated generations to that point, which allowed them to capitalize on many economic and technological shifts.

Despite the awesome earning power of the Baby Boomers, this group of Americans is grossly undersaved. This financial unpreparedness was merely amplified by the global credit crisis; according to the Center for Economic and Policy Research, over 18 percent of Boomers had negative equity in their homes, and Boomers ages 45 to 54 lost an estimated 45 percent of their median net worth, and those ages 55 to 65 lost roughly 38 percent.

The financially vulnerable Baby Boomers are now facing an even worse crisis, as the U.S. government borrows record amounts of debt, thus jeopardizing the Social Security, Medicare, and Medicaid programs. In the United States, Social Security and Medicare currently account for roughly 7 percent of the GDP, but within the next 25 to 30 years these programs will account for nearly 13 percent, essentially the majority of the entire federal budget as Baby Boomers move toward retirement.

The aging crisis in America, and in other developed nations such as the U.K. and of course Japan, will put tremendous strain on an already-weak federal balance sheet. In *The Age of Aging*, UBS Senior Economic Adviser, George Magnus, states:[1]

> *The number of people aged over 60 is expected to reach one billion by 2020 and almost two billion by 2050, some 22 percent of the world's population. In Japan, this age group is expected to double to about 38 percent of the population, only a few percentage points higher than it is expected to be in China. In Europe and America it will account for about 28 percent and 21 percent respectively. And those aged over 80 are expected to account for about 4 percent of the world's population, four times as big as now.*

He continues to write:

> *These changes in age structure are going to lead to significant changes in dependency, which in turn will have enormous economic and financial consequences. Dependency ratios are defined as the number of old or very young people as a percentage of the working age population, that is, those aged 15–64.*
>
> *Most developing countries will still have falling dependency ratios for the next 20 years because youth dependency is falling, and old-age dependency isn't rising especially fast yet. Western countries, on the other hand, have completed the decline in youth dependency and now face a rapid increase in old-age dependency.*

With so much uncertainty in the reliability of government-run social safety nets, many Americans (as well as Europeans and Japanese) must rely on themselves to generate sufficient supplemental income to maintain their standard of living, pay down debts, or someday retire. In many cases, Baby Boomers continue to take care of *their* retired parents and their adult children who continue to live at home. These Kids in Parents' Pockets Eroding Retirement Savings ("KIPPERS," as coined in the U.K.), which is a phenomenon directly attributed to the success of the Baby Boom generation, are merely further strangling a financially strapped demographic that is desperately in need of liquidity.

As health-care costs rise and these Boomers realize that they cannot rely on their children or the government for financial support, they will turn to liquidating assets (that still have value) to fund their health-care and retirement costs. Currently the Boomers are the largest consumers of prescription medication in the United States. Seniors over the age of 65 spend on average $3,899 per year on health care and Boomers will spend roughly 22 percent of the U.S. GDP over the next 10 years to meet their medical needs.

In a post–credit crisis preretirement era, however, Boomers may not have enough time or sufficient capital to earn back the losses they have incurred in their equities and real estate portfolios to budget for increases in medical expenses or retirement costs. This will give rise to one of the greatest bull markets in history—*reverse equity transactions* (i.e., reverse mortgages and the secondary market for U.S. life insurance policies).

REVERSE EQUITY TRANSACTIONS

A *life settlement* is a transaction in which a senior citizen, usually 65 years and older, sells his or her existing life insurance policy to an institutional investor, through a state-licensed intermediary known as a *provider* for more than the cash surrender value but less than the death benefit. The investor makes an offer on the policy based on the expected life expectancy of the individual. Once the transaction is complete, the investor continues to make all future premium payments until the maturity of the policy, at which point the death benefit of the policy is paid out to the investors. The legal foundation for the life settlement market was established in 1911 by Justice Oliver Wendell Holmes, who deemed life insurance an asset similar to real estate, stocks, bonds, or gold, which could be sold to a third party. Holmes wrote about life insurance: "Life insurance has become in our days one of the best recognized forms of investment and self-compelled saving." The life settlement market is currently estimated at roughly $16 billion and is estimated to grow to roughly $160 billion over the next few years, according to Conning Research.

Transactions such as life settlements and reverse mortgages will allow seniors to tap into equity in their homes and life insurance policies that are largely independent from traditional creditworthiness metrics such as FICO credit scores and income levels. These transactions are instead based on the projected life expectancy of the individual(s). Simply put, the shorter the life expectancy for an individual the higher the payment she may receive for her life insurance policy or the higher the amount she may be eligible to borrow from a reverse mortgage.

Although life settlements and reverse mortgages differ in many ways, the longevity-linked asset class offers institutional investors steady returns that are largely uncorrelated to more traditional markets. Life settlements, and synthetic longevity-mortality structures, offer returns almost completely isolated from the real estate, equities, commodities, and bonds markets. Although reverse mortgage investment profits (or losses) are linked directly with the relative value of the underlying homes, the credit rating of the borrowers is not as important as in the traditional mortgage market. Therefore, a portfolio of reverse mortgages or a reverse mortgage–backed security is vulnerable mainly to longevity risk, the risk of longer-living borrowers, and home price risk. A complete list of all associated risk will be discussed in detail later in this book.

Although the concepts of life settlements and reverse mortgages have been in existence for quite some time, these transactions are now more important than ever. Over the next 5 to 10 years, the reverse mortgage will play an increasingly important role in the market for structured financial products and a strong grasp on the part of financial services firms and asset managers of longevity- and mortality-linked securities will be vital to compete in the modern marketplace.

The purpose of this introductory book is to create a foundation for understanding the mechanics of the reverse mortgage transaction (for information on life settlements and longevity finance, please reference *Life Markets: Trading Mortality and Longevity Risk with Life Settlements and Linked Securities*, also published by John Wiley & Sons). The book covers a wide array of reverse mortgage–specific topics from the history, taxation, and actuarial underwriting to the rating methodology and analysis of reverse mortgage–backed securities. Chapters are pulled from the foremost experts in their specific fields and the contributors to book are highly regarded in the longevity/mortality–linked markets.

There are four parts to *Reverse Mortgages and Linked Securities*. Part One provides the reader with a formal introduction to the asset class touching on basic concepts, the history of reverse mortgages, and a discussion of the Home Equity Conversion Mortgage (HECM), which accounts for the majority of loans in the reverse mortgage market today.

Part Two deals with the actuarial underwriting of reverse mortgages and other associated risks. As it is discussed at length in the book, reverse mortgages are actuarially dependent as opposed to credit dependent, so understanding the various methodologies of determining life expectancy is critical. The section also discusses interest rate and housing price risks and also offers up possible risk mitigation solutions. It may be confusing as to why the chapter called "Longevity Risk and Fair Value Accounting" is in Part Two, as opposed to Part Three, but despite the title, the chapter serves in understanding the development of actuarial analysis. Part Two also includes Standard & Poor's rating mythology for reverse mortgage–backed securities, which focuses on the risks of these assets.

Part Three establishes the tax treatment of reverse mortgage borrowers and lenders, and investors in reverse mortgage–backed securities.

Part Four puts reverse mortgages into varying contexts, first discussing the viability of the reverse mortgage product in Japan, and then comparing the economics of reverse mortgages to other products such as life settlements and home equity lines of credit.

Appendix A, "Housing Wealth among the Elderly," is a simple discussion of the wealth possessed by seniors in the United States, Australia, and Japan.

Appendix B, "Reverse Mortgage Analytics," provides another view on the quantitative aspects of reverse mortgages. Although the subject matter in this section is discussed in previous sections, it is isolated in this appendix for quick reference.

At the end of each chapter I provide a very brief commentary on the subject matter discussed by the contributing author. The purpose for doing this is to emphasize certain key points or offer up some further considerations and discussion points.

NOTE

1. George Magnus, *The Age of Aging: How Demographics Are Changing the Global Economy and Our World*, (Hoboken, NJ: John Wiley & Sons, 2008).

Acknowledgments

I would like to thank all of the co-authors who took the time to make highly insightful contributions to the book. Thank you again for helping to shape and nurture the *life markets*.

List of Contributors

Vishaal B. Bhuyan
Managing Director
VB Bhuyan & Co. Inc.

Micah Bloomfield
Partner
Stroock & Stroock & Lavan LLP

Chris DeSilva
Managing Partner
Risk Capital Partners, LLC

Mike Fasano
President
Fasano Associates

Kai Gilkes
Analyst
Standard & Poor's

Victoria Johnstone
Analyst
Standard & Poor's

Apea Koranteng
Analyst
Standard & Poor's

Peter Mazonas
Managing Member
Life Settlement Financial, LLC

Olivia S. Mitchell
Chair, Department of Insurance & Risk Management
The Wharton School, University of Pennsylvania

Karen Naylor
Analyst
Standard & Poor's

Nemo Pererra
Co-Founder & Principal
Risk Capital Partners, LLC

John Piggott
School of Economics
University of New South Wales

Andrea Quirk
Analyst
Standard & Poor's

Joseph R. Selvidio
Associate
Stroock & Stroock & Lavan LLP

Charles Stone
Associate Professor
Brooklyn College
City University of New York
Department of Economics

Boris Ziser
Partner
Stroock & Stroock & Lavan LLP

Anne Zissu
Professor
Citytech
City University of New York
Department of Business
The Polytechnic Institute of New York University
Department of Financial Engineering

PART One

Reverse Mortgage Basics

CHAPTER 1

Reverse Mortgage Primer

Vishaal B. Bhuyan
Managing Partner, V. B. Bhuyan & Co. Inc.

A *reverse mortgage* is a longevity-linked loan that allows senior citizens, age 62 and older, to release the equity in their home without meeting any credit or income requirements. As opposed to traditional mortgages, there is no obligation to repay a reverse mortgage loan until the borrower passes away or no longer uses the home as a primary place of residence. Upon the death of the borrower(s), sale of the home, or breech of contract, the loan plus interest and fees must be repaid by the sale of the home. It is up to the reverse mortgage lender to sell the home at the time of the borrower's death, as the lender is the rightful owner of the residence at that time.

If at the time of loan expiration (death, or sale) the sale price of the home exceeds the loan amount extended to the senior, the senior (if still living) or his or her heirs (if the senior has passed away) will receive the difference in value. If at the time the sale of the home is insufficient to repay the debt, then the lender must take a loss on the transaction or make a claim to the insurer of the loan, which in the case of Home Equity Conversion Mortgages (HECM) is the Department of Housing and Urban Development (HUD). Although there are a number of varying reverse mortgage products in the market, HECM reverse mortgages make up almost 90 percent of the loans in the current marketplace. Other types of reverse mortgages will be described in later chapters.

For seniors, the requirements to obtain a reverse mortgage are fairly simple:

- The person must be at least 62 years of age for an FHA HECM loan; however, this age minimum may be at the discretion of the lender for nonconforming mortgages.

- The senior's home must be owned outright or have an existing mortgage that may be paid off by the proceeds of the reverse mortgage loan at closing.
- The property must be the borrower's primary residence.
- The senior must not be delinquent on any federal debt.
- The senior must participate in a consumer information session given by an approved HECM counselor.

The FHA HECM program will be discussed in further detail in the next chapter, and other agency loans as well as nonconforming jumbo reverse mortgages will be discussed in later chapters; however, the majority of principles apply to both conforming and nonconforming mortgages. Currently, *conforming* mortgages, according to the FHA HECM program, are loans equal to or less than $625,000 (which had been increased from $200,000 to $417,000 in 2008). Conversely, mortgages above $625,000 would be considered *nonconforming*, or *jumbo*, reverse mortgages.

LOAN DISBURSEMENTS

It is important to remember that (FICO) scores and income requirements are *not* a prerequisite for many reverse mortgages, especially HECM loans; however, in the case where the senior moves out of the home, repayment risk does exist. Although the senior is not required to make principal or interest payments on the loan, the borrower(s) are responsible for paying all maintenance costs, homeowners insurance, and property taxes associated with the home. In that respect, it should be noted that a lender should be confident that a borrower has the means to maintain the quality of the property and stay current on all taxes.

Since the credit profile of a borrower is of less importance in a reverse mortgage than in traditional mortgages, there is a significant weight put on the life expectancy of a borrower. Up-to-date and sufficient actuarial data is needed in order to develop accurate pricing models for reverse mortgage loans. Although HUD-insured reverse mortgage loans protect the lender from "longevity risk" (the risk that a borrower lives longer than expected), it is in the best interest of the lender to utilize accurate mortality tables. HECM-issued loans, which are made to seniors age 62 and older, are structured using outdated and inaccurate actuarial data. These loans are priced to be losing investments, no matter whose balance sheet the loss ends up on.

The concept of marrying actuarial underwriting to the capital markets is not new, and is best illustrated in the secondary market for life insurance, where investors analyze pools of life insurance for purchase. These investors are developing increasingly more sophisticated actuarial views. Unfortunately, the reverse mortgage market is lagging behind the life settlements market in this regard. Underwriting will be discussed in detail in Part Three of this book.

In all reverse mortgages, the lender calculates the amount to be disbursed to the senior(s) by considering the following:

- The age and life expectancy of the borrower, or the age of the younger borrower in the case of a married couple.
- Current interest rates. (FHA HECM interest rate calculations will be explained in the next chapter.)
- The appraised value of the home, with consideration of ongoing maintenance costs and geographic location.
- How the loan is to be made to the borrower (i.e., lump sum, credit line, etc.).

Loans may be disbursed to the borrower in a number of ways. Although the FHA offers many types of loan programs, the most common ones are shown in Table 1.1. Private lenders may introduce variations on these programs or entirely new products to the marketplace.

A reverse mortgage loan may be costly for certain seniors. In the case of HECM-insured loans, the borrower's origination and servicing fees are highly regulated and limited in many cases. For example, HECM loans are limited to roughly a $6,000 origination fee, which, at the time of this writing, has been reduced even further. No such cap on origination fees exists in nonconforming reverse mortgage loans, which are not insured by HUD or any other government agency. From an investor's standpoint, this may present a tremendous opportunity in the nonconforming sector of the market, as longevity and real estate risk maybe more favorably and accurately priced.

TABLE 1.1 Reverse Mortgage Disbursement Options—U.S. Department of Housing & Urban Development

Tenure	Equal monthly payments as long as at least one borrower lives and continues to occupy the property as a principal residence.
Term	Equal monthly payments for a fixed period of months selected.
Line of credit	Unscheduled payments or installments, at times and in amounts of your choosing, until the line of credit is exhausted.
Modified tenure	Combination of line of credit with monthly payments for as long as you remain in the home.
Modified term	Combination of line of credit plus monthly payments for a fixed period of months selected by the borrower.

OVERVIEW OF LENDER CHALLENGES

Because senior citizens are responsible for the upkeep of the house they are living in, but do not own, a reverse mortgage can present a lender with a number of challenges. Among those challenges is the case of *default* on the part of the senior. A senior may allow the home's pipes to freeze, landscape to run wild, and roof to weaken without giving much thought to making repairs. Although homeowner's insurance covers the majority of these issues, seniors may still not want to deal with deductible payments or premium increases or may be just generally apathetic to the appearance and structural quality of the home. The senior may even unknowingly fall behind on property taxes or insurance payments. In these very delicate situations, where the senior is in direct breach of the loan agreement, the lender may be forced to remove the senior from his or her home. Clearly, the sight of a sheriff evicting a 75-year-old woman from her home does not sit well with anyone, so careful attention must be given to the systems in place to monitor and manage a portfolio of reverse mortgage loans. Although this ethical and headline risk may not be the norm, it is something all potential reverse mortgage participants should be well aware of.

SUMMARY

Many institutional investors are currently examining various ways to participate in this marketplace, aside from traditional mortgage lenders such as Wells Fargo and Bank of America (Countrywide), which have reverse mortgage platforms. One group, KBC Financial Products, a unit of the Belgium-based KBC Bank, has actively participated in this space by purchasing an entire reverse mortgage lender at one point, and reselling the firm's $800 million reverse mortgage pool in February 2010. Another notable market participant is Knight Capital Group (NASDAQ: NITE), which purchased Urban Financial in March 2010.

The securitization of reverse mortgages is the ultimate "holy grail" that has been eluding both this asset class and other *life-linked* assets such as life settlements. In both cases, with focus on reverse mortgages, the unpredictability of cash flows seems to be one of the most important hurdles to overcome in the structuring of these loans. Although there has been a Ginnie Mae reverse mortgage–backed security, it has experienced limited demand. The development of more widely accepted actuarial and pricing methodologies for reverse mortgages should give rise to a more successfully structured product. This would allow investors to participate in the demographic shifts occurring here in the United States as well as in other parts of the world, such as Japan.

Securitization of reverse mortgages and opportunities for the reverse mortgage product in Japan are both discussed in further detail in later chapters.

CHAPTER 2

The History of Reverse Mortgages: An Insider's View

Peter M. Mazonas
Life Settlement Financial, LLC

The first reverse mortgage–type loans are thought to have been done in Europe, probably France.[1] In French, the system is called *viager*, after a word for "pension." The most famous of these is a lesson in longevity risk. In 1965, Andre-Francois Raffray approached Jeanne Calment and offered her the equivalent of $500 per month for life in exchange for his inheriting her country house when she died. Mr. Raffray was most certainly convinced he had a good deal because at the time, he was 45 years old and Ms. Calment was 90. He died in 1996 at the age of 77 and she outlasted him by two years, dying at 122.

FORMATIVE YEARS

Except for one-off reverse mortgage–type loans in the United States, the first organized reverse mortgage program began in 1963 in Oregon as a property tax deferral program to ease the financial burden for seniors and allow them to remain in their homes. In this case, the Oregon Public Employees' Retirement Fund advanced monies to the seniors with the expectation of repayment when the seniors moved from their homes. State and county government in other states followed suit. These were simple loan programs tied to need and promoted by social responsibility.

In 1979, the San Francisco Development Fund contacted Anthony M. (Tony) Frank, who was then CEO of Nationwide Savings and chairman of the Federal Home Loan Bank board, about creating a pilot *Reverse Annuity Mortgage (RAM)* program. This program was launched in Northern

California and closed the first RAM loan in 1981. Tony was later my partner in creating Transamerica HomeFirst, the private reverse mortgage subsidiary of Transamerica Corporation. The RAM program expanded throughout California in 1982 under the direction of Bronwyn Belling, later the program director at AARP.

Much of the credit for creating the reverse mortgage industry then and for the next 20 years goes to a handful of dedicated people like Ken Scholen, Bronwyn Belling, Don Ralya, Jeff Taylor, and Katrina Smith Sloan at AARP. Although AARP has never endorsed a specific reverse mortgage vendor, they have been the principal sponsor of educational programs and a force in channeling legislation and model statutes in favor of reverse mortgages.

By 1984, the Senate was working on proposals to introduce an FHA reverse mortgage program where the loans would be insured by HUD. It was not until 1987 that the pilot program, called a *Home Equity Conversion Mortgage (HECM)*, was approved and the first loans were written in 1989. In 1990, the pilot program was expanded to a limit of 25,000 loans using FHA loan limits and with a program sunset date of September 31, 1995. In January 1996, the program was extended.

PRIVATE PROGRAMS

The first private reserve mortgage companies and programs began coming to market in 1988. These were typically insurance company–backed operations taking advantage of the insurance carriers' low cost of capital and need for high returns on investment. Among these companies were Capital Holdings, Louisville, Kentucky, and Transamerica, San Francisco, California.

One non-insurance-carrier reverse mortgage startup, Providential Home Income Plan, also from San Francisco, had a meteoric rise to become one of the most successful IPOs in 1992. The company was founded by Bill Texido, a pioneer from the rail car leasing business. Modeled in much the same way as a rail car lease, the product design was all about leverage and fees. However, before the end of the "lockup period," when insiders could start to sell stock, the Company cratered because of a combination of an interest rate mismatch in sourcing and lending of funds, and speculative product design. The combination led to the SEC invoking accounting treatment, which was very unfavorable to the Company and their speculative product design. Providential was borrowing at high interest rates in the short-term market and lending long term at significantly lower interest rates.

Providential's product design was loaded with front-end origination and front-loaded equity sharing fees that the SEC believed unjustly accelerated income (in advance of the planned IPO). On September 2, 1992, the SEC issued an opinion letter stating that reverse mortgages should be accounted for in the same way as annuities.[2] This was one of the first implementations of fair value accounting that required Providential and all other companies to capitalize origination costs and spread them over the life of a hypothetical pool of mortgages.

This SEC ruling meant that aggressive product design was punished and more conservative products received income recognition advantages. When this letter ruling was applied to Providential's pool of loans, it drove their pool internal rate of return below 10 percent. By contrast, the similar, but conservative, product from Transamerica HomeFirst enjoyed an annualized projected rate of return of over 20 percent.

The period in the late 1980s and 1990s saw numerous innovative reverse mortgage product designs. As far back as 1985, Bronwyn Belling and the United Seniors Health Cooperative, Washington D.C., conceptualized a line of credit product. This product design suffered from the same fault as many later programs in that these were loans with fixed terms: 10 years, 20 years. This meant that at some predetermined future date "the bank" would come in and seize the home in the unfortunate case where the senior was still alive and living in the home.

FIRST LIFETIME REVERSE MORTGAGES

This product design flaw was corrected in 1991 when, through Transamerica HomeFirst and Robert Bachman of Home Equity Partners (later called Freedom Financial), I introduced the first lifetime reverse mortgages. Although different in design, they allowed the senior(s) or the surviving senior to remain in the home until they permanently moved out, typically for medical reasons. Home Equity Partners accomplished this by using the proceeds from a private reverse mortgage to buy an immediate annuity that paid the senior(s) income for life. This product design benefited Home Equity Partners because all of the fee income was immediate and got around the SEC ruling. It also eliminated any need for loan servicing by shifting that responsibility to the annuity provider. As with other private reverse mortgage programs, the continued viability was dependent on the issuing insurance company's appetite to stay in the business.

Transamerica HomeFirst's design approach was different. Under Transamerica's lifetime reverse mortgage, "HouseMoney," the senior received monthly payments funded by Transamerica. The initial advance to the senior at the close of escrow include additional funding to purchase a deferred annuity that took over making monthly payments at a predefined point in the future. This point was approximately 18 months before the senior's average life expectancy. By design, this meant that between 60 and 70 percent of seniors purchasing this product would receive the equivalent of their single premium deferred annuity payment back in monthly payments before reaching life expectancy, and then, income for life from the annuity. Another unique feature of the deferred annuity is that the annuity providers, Transamerica and MetLife, issued the annuity directly to the senior with no commission or upfront profit to anyone. The survivors would continue to receive annuity payments for the rest of their lives whether or not they remained in their homes. This patented design offered higher monthly payments because principal payments under the loan were truncated when the annuity took over making the monthly payments.

Despite the elegance of design, this product was criticized because some homeowners died before they began receiving payments from the annuity, thus incurring high front-end loan costs. A second new feature introduced in this product, shared appreciation, also drew fire in lawsuits brought by disgruntled family members. Shared appreciation features were incorporated into FHA and later Fannie Mae reverse mortgages, but these government and quasi-government organizations were not as easy to bring suits against as a publicly traded corporation.

Future home appreciation was used in two ways in Transamerica HomeFirst's Lifetime Reverse Mortgage. First, the appraised home value at time of origination was increased by 2.5 percent compounded annually until the estimated the life expectancy of the homeowner. Inclusion of this future home appreciation meant there was more home value available against which to lend. A loan to a senior with a life expectancy of 10 years meant the senior was given credit for an additional 27 percent home value when the monthly payments were calculated. Because of this risk, the Company had a loan provision that allowed it to share 50/50 with the homeowner in future appreciation at sale in excess of the appraised value of the home at origination. This shared appreciation feature was in lieu of fixed percentage of home value fees used by others, including early Fannie Mae/HUD HECM reverse mortgage products.

Transamerica HomeFirst wrote these shared appreciation Lifetime Reverse Mortgages through 1998, despite serious home devaluation and a later surge in home values. From 1992 through 1997, housing prices in Los Angeles County declined by over 30 percent. Between 1997 and mid-1998, when the housing markets rebounded, values doubled in Southern California and other markets. By early 2000, home prices doubled again, spawning a rash of lawsuits over the shared appreciation feature. Although the defendants never lost a suit, the Company usually settled out of court. One case went to trial in 2004, with the final decision on behalf of the defendants being upheld by the California Court of Appeals in September 2006—seven years after the first lawsuit.

During this same period, private reverse lenders and HUD/HECM introduced line-of-credit loan programs giving seniors the opportunity to draw down home value in the same way younger homeowners could with conventional home equity loans. Lower front-end fees and the ability to create a "rainy-day reserve" made these programs popular. *Popular*, however, is a relative term. Prognostications that reverse mortgages would become a popular and common financial planning tool by the year 2000, and certainly by 2010, were optimistic. In fact, Reverse Mortgage Insights, Inc. (www.rminsight.net) has calculated that in 2009, reverse mortgages had tapped into only 2 percent of the total possible market. This lack of product acceptance has deep roots seeded in the Great Depression and nurtured by reports of fraud, abuse, and the lack of broad education about reverse mortgages.

Ignorance of education about reverse mortgages was not due to lack of effort to educate. As in all markets dealing with seniors, consumer protection was an early consideration. Independently and later sponsored by AARP, Ken Scholen and others wrote books, articles, and scholarly papers about the advantages and pitfalls of reverse mortgages. In 1995, AARP distributed 400,000 copies of the fifth edition of Ken Scholen's "Home-Made Money" (http://assets.aarp.org/www.aarp.org_/articles/revmort/home MadeMoney.pdf). This was timed to coincide with the Congressional decision to extend the HECM "pilot" program due to expire at the end of 1995.

FANNIE MAE STAKES A CLAIM TO THE MARKETPLACE

The 1996 extension of the HUD/HECM program ushered in the large-scale opportunity for mortgage brokers to begin promoting and offering these government-guaranteed reverse mortgages. The brokers offered these loans through a program backed by Fannie Mae with a HUD guarantee. At the same time, county and state programs started offering reverse mortgage counseling to prospective borrowers. This counseling was later mandated by the federal government as much to combat fraud and abuse as to educate.

In 1996, Fannie Mae introduced a proprietary "Home Keeper" reverse mortgage program. Fannie Mae is a *government-sponsored entity (GSE)*, a government-chartered mortgage broker and clearinghouse. The Home Keeper product had higher loan limits than the HUD HECM. These higher limits were based on the borrower's county FHA loan limits for single-family homes, often significantly higher than the HECM loan limits. These were often twice the loan limits set for HECM reverse mortgages. Although the Home Keeper loans did not enjoy the HUD/taxpayer guarantees of the HECM program, this meant little to the borrower in these nonrecourse loans. The Home Keeper loans allowed condominium owners to now take out a reverse mortgage, as well as allowing homeowners to leverage equity in their first residence in order to purchase a new home.

The modest downside of the Home Keeper program was that the loan advances to couples were less than those to single borrowers. In the HECM and most other programs, the available loan limits were calculated based on the mortality table life expectancy of the younger spouse.

ROOTS OF THE SECURITIZATION OF REVERSE MORTGAGES

Little known, but extremely important to the expansion of the Fannie Mae reverse mortgage program was the 1994 requirement by Congress that by the year 2000, 25 percent of all Fannie Mae loans needed to be in the "low-income" category. Barry Abbott of Howard Rice, a San Francisco law firm, and I successfully lobbied the Federal Reserve to have reverse mortgages recategorized as low-income loans under the reasoning that many seniors lived on low fixed incomes. Our simple goal was to expand the market for all reverse mortgages. Fannie Mae used this opportunity to expand the upper limit of the FHA conforming loan limit from $203,150 in 1994 to $362,790 in 2008. Congress in raising this loan limit allowed Fannie Mae to control much of the conventional forward and reverse mortgage markets with their Home Keeper program. The Home Keeper program was discontinued in September 2008, when Congress doubled the FHA loan limit to $729,750 and included HECM loans in the category available to utilize this limit. Reflecting back, we and others in this lobbying effort never imagined the "low-income" category would morph by 2004 into the Fannie Mae securitization of conforming subprime and adjustable ARM loans to truly low-income Americans. Few understood that Fannie Mae was to become a mortgage securitization powerhouse.

Fannie Mae had one great advantage over private reverse mortgage lenders: the federal government's balance sheet. At that time, Transamerica Corp. was a $60 billion company that had been successfully operating in the low-cost commercial paper markets since 1948. Transamerica HomeFirst was able to utilize this low-cost source of capital. Fannie Mae, an entity created by the federal government and backed by the government's financial strength, had access to capital at 50 basis points (0.5 percent) less than HomeFirst's cost of capital. This pricing advantage and early design flaws in the HECM program allowed Fannie Mae to create products that offered seniors more money per month than private lenders. Then, as today, the reverse mortgage business was all about how much money an individual lender can offer a senior. Today this is accomplished by small product differences lenders use to differentiate their HUD-guaranteed products.

Fannie Mae had another distinct advantage that still exists. Borrowers pay a mortgage insurance premium at the time their loan is originated. These premiums, in theory, were thought to be sufficient to offset HUD's guarantee to Fannie Mae to take back, "put," all loans that went under water. When the sum of the principal advances and accumulated compound loan interest exceeds the origination loan amount, each reverse mortgage is surrendered to HUD and the American taxpayers absorb the loss with more national debt resulting. As time has gone on and long-lived Fannie Mae reverse mortgages have reached that tipping point, the volume of losses now exceeds the capacity of the mortgage insurance pool to cover the losses. In 1994, when I pointed this out to my partner, Tony Frank, who had been Postmaster General from March 1988 through July 1992, Tony remarked, "That problem will not come home to roost for two administrations, and that is a long time in Washington."

Then, as now, reverse mortgages were a hard social sell. Seniors spend their whole lives working to pay off their forward home mortgage only to be offered "the opportunity" to reverse mortgage that home. This stigma was particularly important in the early days when most reverse mortgage borrowers were children of the Great Depression. These were the *savers* who educated their children and provided them opportunities never available in their own youth. Most early reverse mortgages were entered into out of need, not as a conscious planning tool. This use of reverse mortgages to avert a crisis opened the door for mortgage brokers and family members to take advantage of senior homeowners. Although government-mandated educational materials were available at no charge, brokers would exact cash payments to distribute materials and require front-end cash payments to take applications. The hangover from these practices is still with the industry today.

In 1997, Jeffrey Taylor organized the National Reverse Mortgage Lenders Association (NRMLA). Jeff had spent the preceding years running a large mortgage and reverse mortgage servicing company and knew the need for the reverse mortgage industry to self-regulate. Jeff was the founder of Wendover Funding Inc., which was the first lender to offer wholesale access to the reverse mortgage business for the HECM HUD reverse mortgage product. He retired from Wendover Funding in 1999, and was recruited by Wells Fargo to build its reverse mortgage sales and servicing operation. Wells Fargo is the largest retail reverse mortgage originator in the United States. Mr. Taylor retired from Wells Fargo in August 2009 and is now chairman of RMInsight Inc., a reverse mortgage data performance company.

By this time, private reverse mortgage programs were giving way to the HECM and Home Keeper programs. Transamerica HomeFirst discontinued its captive sales force HouseMoney program in 1998. Clearly, HECM and Home Keeper loans sold by large and small mortgage broker organizations that could cross-sell would be the trend in the future. In 2000, Financial Freedom merged with Unity Mortgage to become the largest reverse mortgage brokerage. It was quickly overtaken by Wells Fargo Bank and Bank of America. The appeal is that reverse mortgages offer strong fee revenue to brokerages that can leverage their branches and existing marketing programs. There is little incentive for these mortgage powerhouses to create proprietary private reverse mortgage programs when the FHA limit is at $729,750. Even if this limit is reduced back down to $362,790, except for housing on both coasts, these limits cover most of the housing stock in the United States.

In 1989, Joe Torrence introduced to me the concept of securitizing reverse mortgages. Joe had been a managing director at Lehman Brothers and later shared management responsibilities at Fannie Mae with James Johnson and Michael Rush. Joe was later recruited to create GMAC Commercial Mortgage. The securitization model was to use a rated zero-coupon bond where the loan maturities would fund the ongoing obligation to make loan payments to borrowers. Provided each loan in the pool was properly underwritten to control longevity risk and interest rate risk was controlled, the tail risk was minimal and did not require either private or public mortgage insurance. Because Transamerica Corp. agreed to provide the funding for all loans, securitization was never implemented. It would be 15 years before the securitization concept would reemerge.

In early 2009, Fannie Mae stopped securitizing reverse mortgages. This meant that Wells Fargo and Bank of America had to step in to perform this function. They are allowed to incorporate Ginnie Mae/FHA guarantees into these securitizations. The government has increased the capital requirements for firms to participate in underwriting these securities. This will further limit the participants to large financial institutions.

SUMMARY

After 30 years, reverse mortgages have managed to penetrate only 2 percent of the possible market for this novel and useful financial planning tool. Why is this so? The upper loan limits are sufficient to exclude only high-priced homes on either coast. Advertising, loan counseling, and other out-reach efforts have gotten the word out, but seniors are still resisting. The spending habits of today's seniors are greatly affected by their having been teenagers during the Great Depression. Not until reverse mortgage products and their pricing fundamentally change will reverse mortgages become the financially helpful tool many in the industry hope for.

BHUYAN'S FINAL POINTS

- The reverse mortgage product is not a new financial instrument; it has been in existence for more than 30 years.
- Despite their long history, reverse mortgages have experienced limited consumer acceptance.
- New products need to be developed to pique the interest of seniors and financial institution. These products must both be fee friendly for seniors, and accurately reflect the longevity risk for institutional investors.
- The post–credit crisis economy has set the stage for a reverse mortgage rebirth.

NOTES

1. A chronological point-by-point history of the reverse mortgage industry can be found at www.reverse.org/History.HTM.
2. A copy of the original September 2, 1992 letter from SEC Chief Accountant Walter Schutze to Providential can be found at www.lifesettlementfinancial.com/articles.html.

CHAPTER 3

HECM Explained

Reverse Mortgages Originated via the Home Equity Conversion Mortgage (HECM) Program

Boris Ziser
Partner, Stroock & Stroock & Lavan LLP

Joseph R. Selvidio
Associate, Stroock & Stroock & Lavan LLP

In the United States today, the number of retired citizens is growing significantly. According to census data, by 2010, over 40 million people will be over the age of 65, a number expected to more than double by 2040.[1] As this retirement community grows, the market for financial products that can provide opportunities to its members to supplement their personal wealth will grow as well. It is also likely that the demand for these kinds of financial products will grow even stronger in light of the difficult economic environment that began in 2008 and has plagued the financial markets in recent times.

One financial product with a potential for growth because of the options it provides to consumers is the reverse mortgage. The reverse mortgage is a tool allowing a homeowner to convert his or her home into cash without the need to meet financial credit checks such as FICO scores and, except in limited circumstances, without the need to repay the lender until the homeowner dies or permanently moves out of the home.[2]

Presently, over 90 percent of the reverse mortgage marketplace is comprised of loans originated through the Home Equity Conversion Mortgage ("HECM") program.[3] This chapter explains the details of HECM (pronounced, *Heckem*), including how the program works and who may qualify as a borrower. Also included is an analysis of whether certain policy changes that followed enactment of the Housing and Economic Recovery Act of 2008 (the "2008 Act") will expand the program's potential for growth.

LEGISLATIVE HISTORY AND PROGRAM FUNDAMENTALS

HECM was created through the enactment of the Housing and Community Development Act of 1987, Section 255 of the National Housing Act (the "1987 Act"). The 1987 Act authorized the Department of Housing and Urban Development ("HUD"), which is the department charged with administering the program, to insure 2,500 HECM loans. Because of the limited size of the program, participating lenders were chosen through a reservation system among the 10 HUD regions across the country.[4]

The program has been expanded over time, and the lender reservation system was subsequently terminated. All Federal Housing Administration ("FHA") approved lenders are now eligible to participate in the HECM program.[5] The HECM program was designated a permanent HUD program in 1998, and origination has increased steadily since that time.[6]

Like other reverse mortgages, a HECM loan allows a homeowner to obtain a nonrecourse loan secured by the value of his or her home.[7] As long as a borrower pays taxes, keeps his or her home in good order, and maintains the requisite level of property insurance, the loan does not have to be repaid until the borrower (or, if there are two borrowers, until the second of the two borrowers) dies or permanently moves out of the house.[8] Because of this repayment structure, the lender's ability to be repaid for the loan does not depend on the homeowner's creditworthiness, and, as such, a HECM borrower does not need to satisfy financial preconditions in order to qualify for the program. The absence of a stated maturity date for these loans, and the absence of a creditworthiness test for these borrowers, are the two major qualities that distinguish HECM loans from other types of home equity loans.[9]

A hallmark of the HECM program is the FHA-provided insurance coverage each loan receives. As noted previously, for a typical HECM borrower, his or her outstanding loans do not need to be repaid until he or she dies or permanently moves out of the home.[10] These events constitute "maturity" for HECM loans. Because of this, if a lender miscalculates how long it will take before a loan reaches maturity, the loan balance could exceed the fair market value of the home and the lender would not be able to recover amounts owed to it.

The FHA insurance coverage protects lenders against this "longevity" risk in one of two ways. First, if the outstanding balance of the loans, including accrued interest, reaches 98 percent of the maximum amount of funds the lender has committed to make available to a borrower, then the HECM lender may assign the loans to HUD and receive insurance benefits (specifically, an amount equal to the outstanding balance including accrued interest) at that time. Alternatively, if a lender continues to hold the loans for the entire term, but the outstanding amounts due under the loans exceed the property's value at maturity (such difference, the "loan excess"), then the HECM lender may submit a claim to FHA for insurance benefits, which will be in an amount equal to the loan excess.[11]

In addition to protecting lenders against longevity risk, the FHA insurance also provides several other benefits to HECM borrowers. Because of the protection that lenders receive from longevity risk, the insurance coverage allows HECM lenders to loan higher amounts to borrowers.[12] The coverage also guarantees that a borrower will receive the promised loan funds over the life of the loan, regardless of whether he or she lives in the home longer than expected, and regardless of whether the HECM lender goes out of business.[13]

Finally, the coverage ensures that a HECM borrower will not owe more than the value of his or her house at the end of the loan's term.[14] A HECM borrower makes an initial *mortgage insurance premium* payment at closing in an amount equal to 2 percent of the maximum amount of funds the lender has committed to make under the loan. Subsequent mortgage insurance premium payments accrue at an annual rate of one-half of 1 percent of the lender's committed funds. The HECM borrower is responsible for paying one-twelfth of this annual payment on a monthly basis for the term of the loan.[15]

The requirements necessary to qualify as a HECM borrower are relatively straightforward. An individual must be at least 62 years old to participate in the program.[16] The individual's home must either be (1) a single-family dwelling, (2) a multiple family dwelling of four units or less where the borrower is the primary resident in one of the units, or (3) a qualifying condominium or manufactured home.[17] If a HECM borrower has any existing liens against his or her home, these liens must be paid off in full at closing.[18] All borrowers must also agree to meet with an approved HECM counselor prior to closing.[19]

DISBURSING FUNDS AND CALCULATING LOANS AND INTEREST

The maximum amount of funds for which a HECM borrower may qualify is referred to as the "Maximum Claim Amount" ("MCA"). The Maximum

Claim Amount is equal to the lesser of (1) the appraised value of the borrower's home and (2) the FHA's statutorily imposed cap on loan limits.[20] Previously, FHA loan limits were generally set at 95 percent of a county's median house price. The 2008 Act created a national limit for HECMs, which was set at $417,000.[21] The American Recovery and Reinvestment Act of 2009 increased this limit to $625,500, and in October 2009, Congress extended this limit for an additional year.[22]

After the Maximum Claim Amount is determined, the "Initial Principal Limit" ("IPL") is calculated by multiplying the Maximum Claim Amount by a number between zero and one. This number is referred to as the "Principal Limit Factor."[23] The Principal Limit Factor is based on the interest rate applicable to the loans and the age of the borrower. If there is more than one borrower, the age of the youngest borrower will be used for purposes of calculating the Principal Limit Factor. Because the Principal Limit Factor is intended to ensure that an outstanding loan balance is as close to the Maximum Claim Amount as possible at maturity, if all other things are equal, a lower interest rate will cause the Principal Limit Factor to be closer to one, and a younger borrower will cause the Principal Limit Factor to be closer to zero.[24]

The amount of funds a HECM borrower may receive at closing is referred to as the "Net Principal Limit" ("NPL").[25] The Net Principal Limit is calculated by subtracting closing costs and expenses from the Initial Principal Limit. Closing costs and expenses are comprised of (1) an origination fee, (2) administrative costs such as an appraisal, a title search and title insurance, surveys, inspections, recording fees, mortgage taxes and other fees, (3) the Mortgage Insurance Premium, and (4) a servicing fee.[26] An origination fee can be in an amount of up to $2,500 for a home valued at less than $125,000. For homes valued above $125,000, the origination fee can be up to 2 percent of the first $200,000 of the home's value and 1 percent of the balance of the home's value, up to a maximum amount of $6,000.[27] A servicing fee can be no more than $30 per month if the loan has an annually adjusting interest rate and $35 per month if the loan adjusts on a monthly basis.[28]

A HECM borrower can choose to have interest accrue on amounts outstanding under the loans at either a fixed or an adjustable rate. An adjustable interest rate can be reset either monthly or annually, but the interest rate on a HECM loan may not increase more than 2 percent in any one year or more than 5 percent over the term of the loan. A HECM lender will calculate the interest rate applicable to a particular loan based on the United States Treasury Securities rate, plus a margin that is typically between 1 and 2 percent.[29]

A HECM borrower can choose to receive loan disbursements in one of five ways. First, under the "tenure" option, disbursements can be made to a borrower in equal monthly installments for life. The tenure option is sometimes referred to as a *reverse annuity mortgage* because it resembles an annuity product. Second, under the "term" option, a borrower can choose to receive loan disbursements in equal monthly payments for a set term, which the borrower specifies. The end of this term does not trigger "maturity" of the loans, but disbursements will not be made after that time. Third, a borrower can choose to withdraw funds from an available line of credit at unscheduled intervals, from time to time over the life of the loan. Fourth, a borrower can choose to combine receiving equal monthly installments until maturity with access to a line of credit. This is commonly referred to as the *modified tenure* option. Finally, a borrower can choose to combine receiving equal monthly installments for a set term with access to a line of credit, which is referred to as the *modified term* option.[30] A HECM borrower can also modify his or her disbursement options during the life of the loan for an administrative fee of $20.[31]

CHANGES TO THE PROGRAM FOLLOWING THE 2008 ACT

The economic downturn that began in 2008 had an impact on every corner of the credit markets, and the reverse mortgage industry was no exception. However, as the economy recovers, the reverse mortgage is poised to recover as well. In addition to general market conditions that encourage the growth of the reverse mortgage industry (mainly, a growing retirement population and a recovering real estate market to be borrowed against), in passing the 2008 Act, lawmakers have implemented policies intended to grow this marketplace in several ways.

One example is the "HECM for Purchase" program, established by the 2008 Act to allow consumers not only to refinance an existing home, but also to purchase a new home, as well. As another example, the 2008 Act and its related guidelines streamlined the process by which the owners of condominium units may participate in the program.[32]

HECM for Purchase

The HECM program initially was implemented to give consumers the opportunity to remain in their homes during their retirement years.[33] A HECM loan was (and is) a way for a senior to gain access to the equity in his or her home, and to use that equity to offset living expenses like property taxes, insurance, medical expenses and other costs. In establishing the HECM for Purchase program as part of the 2008 Act, Congress created a way to allow seniors to use the HECM program not only to remain in their current homes but also to find new homes more suitable for them during this latter stage of their lives.[34]

The policy behind HECM for Purchase is as follows: Some seniors wish to remain in their current homes for their retirement years, and are looking for a way to access the liquidity in these homes to offset living expenses. For these individuals, the program as it existed prior to the enactment of the 2008 Act was sufficient.

Other seniors, however, wish to find new homes that are smaller, handicapped accessible, closer to friends and family, or located in warmer parts of the country. For this latter category of seniors, participating in the HECM program prior to the existence HECM for Purchase involved a multiple-step process. First, an individual had to sell his or her home and use the proceeds from that sale to pay off any existing mortgage and to make a down payment on a new home. At the closing for the new home, the individual had to take out a traditional, forward mortgage to help pay for the property. Only after this process was complete could the individual start the process of applying for a HECM loan and, ultimately, participate in yet another closing. At the HECM closing, loan proceeds were used to pay off the forward mortgage, and the first and second HECM liens were then recorded against the property.

This structure discouraged some seniors from considering a move because these individuals would not qualify for a traditional, forward mortgage. The structure discouraged other seniors from moving because they were not interested in the time (and expense) required for the additional step of paying off the forward mortgage and participating in the HECM program.

The HECM for Purchase program is designed to encourage seniors to buy new homes by streamlining the closing process. Seniors considering moving can use the proceeds of a HECM loan at the closing for the new home.[35] There is no need to take out a forward mortgage that is only to be paid off in a second closing. As with all HECM loans, the traditional process of obtaining a FICO score and reviewing the borrower's financial history is not required for the HECM for Purchase closing.

Although the HECM for Purchase program is relatively new (taking effect in January 2009), available data suggests that seniors have been interested in participating. Through September 2009, 550 seniors had closed on loans originated through the program. Companies have also started offering HECM for Purchase continuing education programs for realtors, which will increase marketplace awareness of the program and could further facilitate its growth.[36]

To qualify as a borrower under the HECM for Purchase program, an individual must be purchasing a home that will be used as his or her primary residence, and must move into the home no more than 60 days after closing. After closing, the HECM first and second liens must be the only encumbrances against the home. Certain types of properties, such as cooperative units, new construction where a certificate of occupancy (or its equivalent) has not been issued, boarding houses, bed-and-breakfasts, and certain types of manufactured homes, do not qualify for the HECM for Purchase program.[37] Other requirements applicable under the traditional HECM program will also apply to HECM for Purchase transactions.

Revised Condominium Guidelines

Also under the authority of the 2008 Act, in November 2009 HUD issued new guidelines designed to streamline the process by which a senior may obtain a HECM loan on a residential condominium unit. Mortgage Letter 2009-46 B ("Letter 46B"), which took effect on December 7, 2009, and applies both to forward and reverse HUD-insured mortgages, revised and consolidated existing guidance on how condominium projects can receive HUD approval.

Letter 46B gives lenders two options to be used in gaining project approval. The first option is to pursue the HUD Review and Approval Process ("HRAP"). This process was the traditional means of gaining project approval before Letter 46B was issued. Alternatively, lenders who have received an unconditional "Direct Endorsement" from HUD, and who have staff with expertise in reviewing and approving condominium projects, may pursue the Direct Endorsement Lender Review and Approval Process ("DELRAP").

The balance of Letter 46B provides an outline of how projects may be approved under the DELRAP. Included in this outline are details regarding what constitutes an "eligible project," what kinds of conditions must be avoided or mitigated in order to gain project approval (such as noise issues, environmental issues, or a property's proximity to highways, railways, or air fields), and what minimum insurance coverage will be required.

On the same day that Letter 46B was issued, HUD also issued Mortgagee Letter 2009-46 A ("Letter 46A"). This second letter temporarily modifies some of the guidelines included in Letter 46B. Effective from December 7, 2009, through December 31, 2010, these modifications are designed to serve as a "temporary directive to address current market conditions."

For example, while Letter 46B generally prohibits the FHA from insuring more than 30 percent of the units in any one condominium development, Letter 46A increases this concentration level to 50 percent. Although Letter 46B requires that at least 50 percent of the units in a development be either owner occupied or sold to individuals intending to occupy a unit,

Letter 46A excludes certain types of units (such as vacant or tenant-occupied real estate owned) from this calculation.[38] Similarly, although Letter 46B requires that at least 50 percent of the units in a development be sold before any unit receives HUD approval, Letter 46A reduces this requirement to 30 percent.[39] Also under Letter 46A, condominiums located in the State of Florida are not eligible for approval by using the DELRAP.

CONSUMER-FOCUSED ELEMENTS OF THE PROGRAM

Thus far, in this chapter we have discussed how the HECM program began, how it has traditionally operated, and how it will operate in the future in light of the policy changes implemented by the 2008 Act and its regulations and guidelines. Another critical component of the HECM program is the procedure by which it protects consumers seeking to participate in it. Regulators have commented that the reverse mortgage marketplace combines a vulnerable class of consumers (specifically, senior citizens) with a complex financial product and a lending structure that uses nontraditional underwriting that relies heavily on the value of collateral.[40] For this reason, effective regulation that deters predatory lending practices without unnecessarily burdening the marketplace is critical.

In June 2009, John C. Dugan, Comptroller of the Currency, presented remarks to the American Bankers Association entitled, "Consumer Protections for Reverse Mortgages." Later that same month, the Government Accountability Office published a report entitled "Reverse Mortgages: Product Complexity and Consumer Protection Issues Underscore Need for Improved Controls over Counseling for Borrowers" (the "GAO Report"). Included as an appendix to the GAO Report were comment letters from a number of regulators, including the Board of Governors of the Federal Reserve System, the Federal Deposit Insurance Corporation, and Comptroller Dugan's office.[41] These comment letters were submitted in response to an earlier draft of the GAO Report that had been circulated to these regulators before the final draft was published. Comptroller Dugan's remarks, together with the GAO Report and its related comment letters, suggest that in the future, the HECM program will be modified in at least three ways as it relates to consumers.

First, regulators will review marketing materials of reverse mortgage lenders (including HECM lenders) with increased scrutiny.[42] Currently, several regulatory agencies have authority over reverse mortgage marketing materials. At the federal level, the Federal Trade Commission regulates the "unfair or deceptive acts or practices" of non-bank financial companies like mortgage brokers. The Board of Governors of the Federal Reserve System, the Federal Deposit Insurance Corporation, the Office of Comptroller of the Currency, the Office of Thrift Supervision, and the National Credit Union Association all have varying degrees of regulatory authority over federally regulated banks. State banking regulators have similar authority over state-regulated lenders, including those that offer HECM loans.[43]

The GAO Report found that despite (or perhaps because of) the amount of regulatory authority over reverse mortgage marketing practices, a number of lenders had published materials that were potentially misleading to consumers, and regulators had not investigated these materials. In some cases, these materials misrepresented the cost of a HECM loan, or the circumstances by which these loans must be repaid. In other cases, these materials suggested that a HECM loan was closer to a "government benefit" than a loan.[44]

In his remarks to the American Banker's Association, Comptroller Dugan stated that his office would be working with other federal and state regulators to develop "inter-agency guidance" on consumer protections relating to reverse mortgages.[45] If successful in developing this inter-agency guidance, regulators will have a means of establishing how the publication of reverse mortgage materials can be best monitored. Even if the inter-agency guidance is not developed, it is likely that in the regulatory environment that follows the financial crisis of 2008, regulators will police these materials with increased scrutiny.

A second change to the administration of the HECM program will relate to the cross-selling of financial products.[70] In obtaining a reverse mortgage, a consumer gains access to a significant amount of cash, and both Comptroller Dugan and the GAO Report noted that the availability of this cash presents a risk that a lender will seek to sell a consumer other financial products, such as life insurance or annuities, in connection with a HECM loan. A lender may also require the purchase of one or more of these products as a precondition to receiving approval for a HECM loan.[46] Historically, life insurance and annuities have fallen under the regulatory authority of state insurance departments. However, the 2008 Act granted authority to HUD to regulate the cross-selling of financial products in connection with HECM loans.[47] At the time the GAO Report was published, HUD was in the early stages of drafting administrative rules dealing with the cross-selling of financial products in this context.

The GAO Report also found that, in many cases, the counseling a HECM borrower is required to receive prior to closing was insufficient.[48] The GAO Report found that some counselors failed to cover all of the required topics during the counseling session. It also found that some counselors overstated the length of their counseling sessions or failed to adequately assess a consumer's ability to pay the counseling fee. In response to the GAO Report, HUD issued new guidelines, effective October 1, 2009, that implement a roster of "approved counselors" and require all HECM counselors to pass an AARP-approved examination.[49] Looking ahead, HUD may implement additional internal controls to ensure that the counseling process is effective.

SUMMARY

There are a variety of factors suggesting that the reverse mortgage marketplace is poised for growth in the years to come. The increasing number of retiring Baby Boomers, many of whom have suffered losses to their personal savings and will be looking for ways to access liquidity in their homes, will place upward pressure on the demand for the product. As the real estate market continues to recover from the recent economic downturn, the value of these retired consumers' homes, as primary collateral for reverse mortgage loans, will increase as well. In addition, the reemergence of the securitization markets could enable capital markets investors to provide an influx of capital for this marketplace, which would further contribute to its growth.

As the market leader for reverse mortgages, the HECM program stands to benefit from each of these factors. However, the expansion of the reverse mortgage industry will not come without challenges. For one thing, the HECM program is expensive. The Mortgage Insurance Premium, combined with the origination fee, the servicing fee, and other closing costs and expenses, serves as a disincentive for some consumers, especially those applying for smaller amounts of HECM loans. The 2008 Act's cap on origination fees was designed to address the question of costs.[50] As the industry continues to develop, and as greater numbers of non-HECM lenders enter the marketplace, there will be additional pressure to seek ways to reduce program costs.

Additionally, in September 2009, HUD issued Mortgagee Letter 2009-34 ("Letter 34"), which adjusted how the Principal Limit Factor is to be calculated. According to an actuarial analysis prepared for HUD, the Letter 34 methodology will reduce average principal limits under the HECM program by 10 percent.[51] This policy change may have been fueled in part by political and economic realities. Starting in fiscal year 2009, the reserve fund through which HECM loans are insured is the FHA's Mutual Mortgage Insurance ("MMI") Fund.[52] By the fall of 2009, the MMI Fund, which has a Congressional mandate to maintain reserves above 2 percent, had fallen to an all-time low of 0.53 percent.[53] Some commentators view

Letter 34 as one of several underwriting policy changes implemented to reduce potential risk associated with HUD insured loans. Reducing the amount of principal available to a HECM borrower also reduces the likelihood that his or her loan will exceed the Maximum Claim Amount and subsequently result in claim liability for HUD. Regardless of the motivation behind Letter 34, if all other things remain equal, its impact will result in smaller loans being made available to borrowers under the HECM program. Higher interest rates or higher lender spreads would also result in smaller amounts of principal available to borrowers under the program.

Finally, the reverse mortgage industry is a relatively new asset class within the capital markets, and ensuring the integrity of the underlying asset will be critical to getting investors comfortable with reverse mortgages as a product. Recent focus on advertising, cross-selling of financial products, and counseling within the marketplace are steps intended to ensure that HECM reverse mortgages are marketed only to consumers who are suited for the product. Because the HECM program is now insured through the MMI Fund, the 1990 National Affordable Housing Act requires an independent annual actuarial analysis of the program.[54] This yearly actuarial review, the first of which was completed in 2009, will provide considerable

---

BHUYAN'S FINAL POINTS

- HECMs (Home Equity Conversion Mortgages) are administered by the Department of Housing and Urban Development.
- HECM does not depend solely on FICO scores.
- HECM loans comprise roughly 90 percent of the reverse mortgage market.
- HECM limits the loan amounts to $625,000 and limits origination and loan servicing fees.
- As of this writing, initiatives have been taken to substantially reduce origination costs on HECM reverse mortgages.
- HUD-issued mortgage insurance protects lenders from longevity and housing price risk as well as guaranteeing payments to borrowers and ensuring a borrower never owes more than the original loan.
- HECM reverse mortgages are now available to seniors for purchases of new homes.

transparency regarding the size and scope of the HECM program. As long as regulatory oversight is implemented in a way that does not unnecessarily burden the marketplace, it will serve as additional assurance to capital market investors that this industry provides a reputable investment opportunity. As industry documentation is further standardized, and as more market participants develop a track record in the industry, these elements will serve as additional comfort to investors.

NOTES

1. *Reversing the Trend: The Recent Expansion of the Reverse Mortgage Market*, Hui Shan, Federal Reserve Board of Governors (April 2009), at page 4, citing United States Census Bureau data, available at www.census.gov.
2. See generally, the *Department of Housing and Urban Development Handbook*, Section 4235.1, "Home Equity Conversion Mortgages" (the "HUD Handbook"), Section 1-3, "Characteristics of the Mortgage."
3. *Reversing the Trend: The Recent Expansion of the Reverse Mortgage Market*, Hui Shan, Federal Reserve Board of Governors (April 2009), at page 2. See also, "An Actuarial Analysis of FHA Home Equity Conversion Mortgage Insurance Fund Fiscal Year 2009," prepared for U.S. Department of Housing and Urban Development by IBM Global Business Services (October 12, 2009), at page 6. The IBM Global Business Services analysis also notes that the lack of available credit starting in 2008 may have further decreased the availability of proprietary reverse mortgage products. This scenario would suggest that as of calendar year 2009, the HECM program's share of the marketplace likely exceeded 90 percent.
4. HUD Handbook, Section 1-1, "Legislative History," citing the Omnibus Budget Reconciliation Act of 1990 (P.L. 101-508, 11/5/90)).
5. HUD Handbook, Section 1-1, "Legislative History."
6. According to information published by the *Wall Street Journal*, in March and April 2009, origination of HECM loans increased 20 percent compared to the same period in 2008. See "Seniors Drawn to Mortgages that Give Back," by Nick Timiraos, June 10, 2009. The article further states that the 11,660 HECM loans originated in April 2009 was the highest monthly total since the program began. According to an actuarial report on the HECM program, it is estimated that insurance-in-force for the HECM program will increase from $28.7 billion in 2009 to $162 billion in 2016. See "An Actuarial Analysis of FHA Home Equity Conversion Mortgage Insurance Fund Fiscal Year 2009," prepared for U.S. Department of Housing and Urban Development by IBM Global Business Services (October 12, 2009), at page i.
7. HUD Handbook, Section 1-3, "Characteristics of the Mortgage." Because the amount of a borrower's equity in his or her home is reduced as additional loan amounts are drawn, reverse mortgages are commonly referred to as "rising debt, falling equity" loans. See generally, GAO Report to Congressional Requesters, "Reverse Mortgages: Product Complexity and Consumer Protection Issues

Underscore Need for Improved Controls over Counseling for Borrowers," GAO-09-606 (June 2009) (the "GAO Report"), at page 4.

8. GAO Report to Congressional Requesters, "Reverse Mortgages: Product Complexity and Consumer Protection Issues Underscore Need for Improved Controls over Counseling for Borrowers," GAO-09-606 (June 2009) (the "GAO Report"), at page 4. See also related "Testimony Before the Special Committee on Aging," U.S. Senate, GAO-09-812T (the "GAO Testimony").

9. While data suggests that the origination of HECM loans has been increasing over time, recent data shows that market conditions have adversely impacted traditional home equity lines of credit. By some estimates, the number of home equity loans made in the first quarter of 2009 was down about 70 percent as compared to the first quarter of 2009. See "Seniors Drawn to Mortgages that Give Back," by Nick Timiraos, June 10, 2009.

10. As stated earlier, a HECM borrower will be required to pay property taxes, maintain insurance coverage, and maintain the house in good order during this time.

11. See generally, HUD Handbook, Section 1-11, "Insurance Options."

12. GAO Report at page 4.

13. GAO Report at page 9. The GAO Report noted that HUD estimates suggest about 25 percent of HECM loans made in a given year will subsequently be assigned to it.

14. GAO Report at page 9. When a HECM loan becomes due, the borrower or his or her heir may retain ownership of the home and repay all amounts outstanding under the loan. However, if the house is sold, the borrower or the heir will not be required to pay any loan amounts above the sale price of the home.

15. HUD Handbook, Section 1-10, "Mortgage Insurance Premium (MIP)." This amount may be paid in cash at closing or added to the outstanding balance of the loan.

16. HUD Handbook, Section 1-3(G), "Characteristics of the Mortgage," Eligibility Requirements. See also, "Top Ten Things to Know if You're Interested in a Reverse Mortgage," available at www.hud.gov.

17. HUD Handbook, Section 3-4, "Eligible Properties." For the HECM for Purchase program, which is discussed later, the Maximum Claim Amount is the lesser of the appraised value of the home, the actual purchase price for the home, and the FHA statutory limit. See generally, "HECM for Purchase Frequently Asked Questions," available at www.hud.gov.

18. HUD Handbook, Section 4-7, "Required Mortgage Credit Documentation."

19. HUD Handbook, Section 1-9, "Counseling." As discussed further in the following, the counseling requirements for the HECM program were revised substantially in November 2009. See HUD Mortgagee Letter 2009-47.

20. HUD Handbook, Section 3-8, "Maximum Claim Amount," as modified by the American Recovery and Reinvestment Act of 2009.

21. GAO Report at page 5. See also, Housing Economic Recovery Act of 2008, Section 1124, "Conforming Loan Limits."

22. GAO Report at page 5. See also, "Extended HECM Loan Limit," by Brian Collins in the *Home Equity Wire* (November 15, 2009), available at

www.nationalmortgagenews.com/hew/. Without this extension, the FHA loan limit would have been reduced to $417,000 in January 2010.

23. HUD Handbook, Section 5-6, "Determining the Borrower's Principal Limit." As discussed, the methodology by which the Principal Limit Factor is calculated was revised in September 2009, and this change is expected to reduce the principal available to HECM borrowers under the program by 10 percent. See HUD Mortgagee Letter 2009-34.

24. *Reversing the Trend*, at page 10.

25. HUD Handbook, Section 5-7, "Determining the Net Principal Limit."

26. GAO Report at page 10. See also HUD Handbook, Section 6-13, "Third Party Fees."

27. GAO Report at page 10. The $6,000 cap on origination fees was implemented by the 2008 Act. See Section 2122 of the 2008 Act, "Home Equity Conversion Mortgages."

28. HUD Handbook, Section 1-12, "Servicing."

29. HUD Handbook, Section 1-8, "Interest Rate." See also *Reversing the Trend*, at page 10.

30. HUD Handbook, Section 5-3, "Payment Plans." As with all payment options, the loan disbursements remain contingent upon the borrower's ability to continue to maintain the home in good order, and to make the required tax and insurance payments.

31. HUD Handbook, Section 5-4, "Changing Payment Plans." See also, "FHA Reverse Mortgages (HECMs) for Consumers," available at www.hud.gov.

32. See generally, the Housing Economic Recovery Act of 2008, Section 2122, "Home Equity Conversion Mortgages." See also Mortgagee Letter 2009-46 A, published by HUD on November 6, 2009 and Mortgagee Letter 2009-46 B, published by HUD on November 6, 2009.

33. HUD Handbook, Section 1-2, "Purpose of the Program" ("The program insures what are commonly referred to as reverse mortgages, and is designed to enable elderly homeowners to convert the equity in their homes to monthly streams of income and/or lines of credit.").

34. See generally, the Housing Economic Recovery Act of 2008, Section 2122, "Home Equity Conversion Mortgages." The 2008 Act reads in relevant part as follows:

(m) Authority To Insure Home Purchase Mortgage—(1) IN GENERAL— Notwithstanding any other provision of this section, the Secretary may insure, upon application by a mortgagee, a home equity conversion mortgage upon such terms and conditions as the Secretary may prescribe, when the home equity conversion mortgage will be used to purchase a 1- to 4-family dwelling unit, one unit of which the mortgagor will occupy as a primary residence, and to provide for any future payments to the mortgagor, based on available equity, as authorized under subsection (d)(9).

35. Housing Economic Recovery Act of 2008, Section 2122.

36. "Generation Mortgage Offers First Continuing Education Course for California Realtors on HECM for Purchase," published in *Real Estate & Investment Business* (August 29, 2009).

37. "HECM for Purchase Frequently Asked Questions," available at www.hud.gov.
38. *Real estate owned (REO)* is a class of property owned by a lender after an unsuccessful foreclosure auction.
39. Letter 46B also eliminates the concept of "spot loan" approval, pursuant to which an individual condominium unit can receive HUD approval prior to the entire condominium project receiving this approval. Letter 46A delays the elimination of the spot loan approval process until February 1, 2010.
40. Remarks by John C. Dugan, Comptroller of the Currency, before the American Bar Association *Regulatory Compliance Conference*, Orlando, Florida, "Consumer Protections for Reverse Mortgages," at page 2 (June 8, 2009) (the "Dugan Remarks").
41. See generally, the GAO Report. Comptroller Dugan's comment letter is dated June 19, 2009.
42. See GAO Report at page 48:

    To enhance consumer protection from potentially misleading marketing, we recommend that the Secretary of the Department of Housing and Urban Development; Chairman of the Federal Trade Commission; Chairman of the Federal Deposit Insurance Corporation; Chairman of the Board of Governors of the Federal Reserve System; Comptroller of the Currency, Office of the Comptroller of the Currency; and Director of the Office of Thrift Supervision, take steps, as appropriate, to strengthen oversight and enhance industry and consumer awareness of the types of marketing claims that we discuss in this report.

    See also Dugan's Remarks at page 10, noting that the OCC will use its authority "to require immediate correction of any potentially misleading marketing claims by a bank in connection with reverse mortgage products, in particular ones that use terms such as 'income for life,' 'no payments ever,' and 'no risk.'"
43. See GAO Report, pp. 15–18.
44. See GAO Report, pp. 19–24. From from page 24: ". . . our research showed that potentially misleading claims exist in the marketplace, which suggests that some HECM providers may not be sufficiently considering federal marketing standards in designing their marketing materials. We referred the claims we identified to FTC or the appropriate federal banking regulator for further review."
45. See Dugan's Remarks at page 11: ". . . the OCC has been working with the other federal bank regulatory agencies on the Federal Financial Institution Examination Council to develop supervisory guidance on reverse mortgages."
46. Conditioning HECM approval on the purchase of other financial products is expressly prohibited by the 2008 Act, which reads in part as follows:

    (o) Prohibition Against Requirements To Purchase Additional Products— The mortgagor or any other party shall not be required by the mortgagee or any other party to purchase an insurance, annuity, or other similar product as a requirement or condition of eligibility for insurance under subsection (c), except for title insurance, hazard, flood, or other peril

insurance, or other such products that are customary and normal under subsection (c), as determined by the Secretary.

47. Relevant language from the 2008 Act reads as follows:

    (p) Study to Determine Consumer Protections and Underwriting Standards—The Secretary shall conduct a study to examine and determine appropriate consumer protections and underwriting standards to ensure that the purchase of products referred to in subsection (o) is appropriate for the consumer. In conducting such study, the Secretary shall consult with consumer advocates (including recognized experts in consumer protection), industry representatives, representatives of counseling organizations, and other interested parties.

48. For an in-depth discussion of the GAO's findings regarding HECM counseling, see the GAO Report, pp. 30–46 ("HUD's internal controls for HECM counseling do not provide reasonable assurance of compliance with HUD requirements.").

49. See 24 CFR Part 206, "Home Equity Conversion Mortgage (HECM) Counseling Standardization and Roster," printed in the *Federal Register* on September 2, 2009 ("This final rule amends HUD's HECM program regulations by establishing testing standards to qualify individuals as HECM counselors eligible to provide HECM counseling to prospective HECM borrowers. The rule also establishes a HECM Counseling Roster (Roster) of eligible counselors and provides for their removal for cause.")

50. Similarly, because of the increased FHA loan limits, the HECM program is now available to a larger number of consumers seeking "jumbo" loans, many of whom will be less sensitive to these program costs.

51. "An Actuarial Analysis of FHA Home Equity Conversion Mortgage Insurance Fund Fiscal Year 2009," prepared for U.S. Department of Housing and Urban Development by IBM Global Business Services (October 12, 2009).

52. See the 2008 Act, providing that HECM program endorsements are to be transferred from the General Insurance Fund to the MMI Fund in fiscal year 2009. For further discussion of this transfer, see also "An Actuarial Analysis of FHA Home Equity Conversion Mortgage Insurance Fund Fiscal Year 2009," prepared for U.S. Department of Housing and Urban Development by IBM Global Business Services (October 12, 2009).

53. See the November 12, 2009 remarks of HUD Secretary Shaun Donovan to Congress, the text of which is available at www.marketnews.com.

54. See "An Actuarial Analysis of FHA Home Equity Conversion Mortgage Insurance Fund Fiscal Year 2009," prepared for U.S. Department of Housing and Urban Development by IBM Global Business Services (October 12, 2009) at page (i), citing the 1990 National Affordable Housing Act.

Underwriting and Risk Analysis

Underwriting Reverse Mortgages

Michael V. Fasano
President, Fasano Associates

A reverse mortgage is a mortgage loan that a homeowner takes against the market value of his or her home. Payment is made by the lender to the homeowner, and interest accrues on the loan until the homeowner either moves out or dies, at which time the loan plus accrued interest must be paid off. For most reverse mortgage programs, the maximum loan amount to be repaid cannot exceed the then-value of the house.

The attractiveness of a reverse mortgage to a homeowner is that he can cash out value from his home and live in it forever, without taking the risk of borrowing in excess of his equity. If he should sell his home in the future, or when he dies, if the home equity exceeds the loan balance, he or his estate will get the value of that excess. If the loan value exceeds the home value, then his liability is capped at the value of his home equity.

Because of its unique characteristics, underwriting for reverse mortgages is different from underwriting traditional mortgage loans. The borrower's creditworthiness is not a significant consideration. Rather, the lender is concerned about the market value of the home, the likely rate of real estate appreciation, the likely level of interest rates, and how long the borrower is likely to live. The likely rate of real estate appreciation will often be related to the likely level of interest rates and, in most scenarios, the accrued interest on the reverse mortgage loan will exceed the appreciation of the underlying real estate.

Therefore, one of the key variables in evaluating how much can be loaned is how long the borrower is expected to live, that is, his or her *life expectancy*. Despite the significance of life expectancy in this calculation, lenders use surprisingly simple methods to evaluate life expectancy.

UNDERWRITING LIFE EXPECTANCY

Like those people who choose to sell their life insurance policies, most applicants for reverse mortgages will be at retirement age or older. When estimating life expectancy in this over-65 market, it is important to understand the nuances of older-age underwriting.

There are two methodologies used in underwriting life expectancy at the older ages—a modified debit methodology and research-based clinical judgment. The modified debit methodology is used in most instances, and entails the use of mortality tables and assessments of relative mortality.

Analyses are made of the extra mortality associated with various impairments, and this extra mortality is expressed as a percentage of standard, or "normal" mortality. We refer to these percentages as *debits*. For example, if a person has coronary artery disease and diabetes, you might estimate the additional mortality for each of those conditions to be 25 debits. You would therefore add a total of 50 debits to 100 percent to generate a mortality rating of 150 percent—meaning that a person with these conditions would be expected to die at 150 percent, or 1.5, times the death rate of a healthy person. The death rates of a healthy population are reflected in a standard mortality table. Thus, to estimate life expectancy, you would apply the mortality rating for the individual being evaluated to the death (and survival) rates of the appropriate standard mortality table. The resulting likelihoods of survival (and death) would give you the person's life expectancy.

When making these assessments for an older demographic, like that of the reverse mortgage market, it is important to understand the differences in disease patterns as they apply to older ages as contrasted with younger ages. For example, risk factors that are associated with higher mortality for younger people, such as family history of heart attack or elevated cholesterol, are not associated with as much extra mortality for older people, where we typically focus on the underlying impairments, like coronary artery disease, rather than the risk factors that would predict those impairments in a younger person. The relevant risk factors for older people are different from those for younger people. Cognitive function and frailty become more important predictors of mortality as you get older, and older-age underwriting needs to incorporate these differences.

In estimating life expectancy it is also important to take a person's income into account, as we know that, up to a point, people of higher income and wealth tend to have more favorable mortality than less-affluent people. It would be generally easy to estimate the income effect in underwriting reverse mortgages, as the applicant's home value is usually a good proxy for her wealth.

For some of the most complex and severe medical histories, we use research-based clinical judgment, in which we go to the primary research literature for the impairment in question, and apply the mortality curves from the literature to the particular profile of the person being evaluated. These more complex analyses require the most sophisticated of analysts, such as physicians and epidemiologists.

LIFE SETTLEMENT VERSUS REVERSE MORTGAGE UNDERWRITING

The secondary market for life insurance, or the life settlement market, provides a useful basis for reverse mortgage underwriting. In recent years, as more and more seniors have decided to sell their life insurance policies in the secondary market, a significant information base has been developed as to the mortality patterns at the older ages. However, this information has not been used in reverse mortgage underwriting, which has been a far simpler process to date.

SIMPLICITY OF THE CURRENT REVERSE MORTGAGE UNDERWRITING PROCESS

The shorter a person's life expectancy, the more he should be able to borrow against the equity of his home. If, for example, a person has only one year to live, he should be able to borrow more than a person who has 10 years to live, as we can expect that only one year's worth of interest will be added to the loan amount, rather than 10. A greater amount could therefore be lent, with a high likelihood that the lender would recoup the loan amount and accrued interest. Thus, you would expect the underwriting process in the reverse mortgage market to take into account the specifics of a borrower's medical condition, as it does in the secondary market for life insurance.

However, other than age, reverse mortgage underwriting does not take into account any medical information. No attempt is made to determine smoking status, which we know affects life expectancy, nor are medical questions asked. The loan amounts are gender neutral. That is, the same amount would be loaned to a male as to a female, even though we know that men have significantly shorter life expectancies than women. The underwriting is so simplified that there is no variation in loan amount for a single homeowner as compared to a joint owner. This defies logic. The reverse mortgage ultimately becomes due when the last of the joint owners dies. Mathematically, this point in time, or this life expectancy, will always be later than the life expectancy of either of the owners. So, to loan the same amount to a single person as you would to a couple makes no sense.

According to AARP (*Reverse Mortgage Loans: Borrowing Against Your Home*, © 2008 AARP Foundation), the remaining life expectancy assumed for a 75-year-old borrower in a HECM (Home Equity Conversion Mortgage, insured by the Federal Housing Administration) program is 12 years. This is the same value as is published in the U.S. Vital Statistics, provided by the National Center for Health Statistics. (See www.cdc.gov/nchs/nvss/mortality/lewk3.htm.) In other words, no attempt is made to discriminate expected mortality based on the income level and other specifics of the person applying for a loan.

WHY DOES UNDERWRITING MATTER?

The reverse mortgage market is currently estimated to represent less than 1 percent of the overall mortgage market. Clearly, the full potential of this market has not been tapped and, as our population continues to age, this missed opportunity will become larger and larger. One of the reasons the market has been limited is that the available loan amounts are not compelling, which is at least partially related to overly simple underwriting. Better underwriting would make the market more efficient for those seeking to access funds for their retirement. Improved underwriting would allow financial institutions to provide larger loans to the extent they could better understand the risks they are assuming on each applicant.

This is not just a business matter, but a social issue as well. People with terminal conditions should have the option of living their remaining life in the comfort of familiar surroundings. This affects both the quality and the length of their final years. By having an underwriting process that takes into account a person's medically determined life expectancy, we will be able to provide larger reverse mortgages to those who need it the most, that is, those with very short life expectancies.

PROPOSED ELEMENTS OF REVERSE MORTGAGE UNDERWRITING

The cost of obtaining medically based life expectancy estimates is not great. The analysis and the cost of gathering the medical information would be in the range of $500 per applicant. Indeed, a number of underwriting firms offer simplified life expectancy calculators that can be done online, for a cost of perhaps $50 to $75 per evaluation. A simplified calculator could be used for expediency, subject to more complete underwriting for shorter life expectancies.

An example of a currently available online calculator, developed by Fasano Associates, is presented in Figures 4.1 through 4.5.

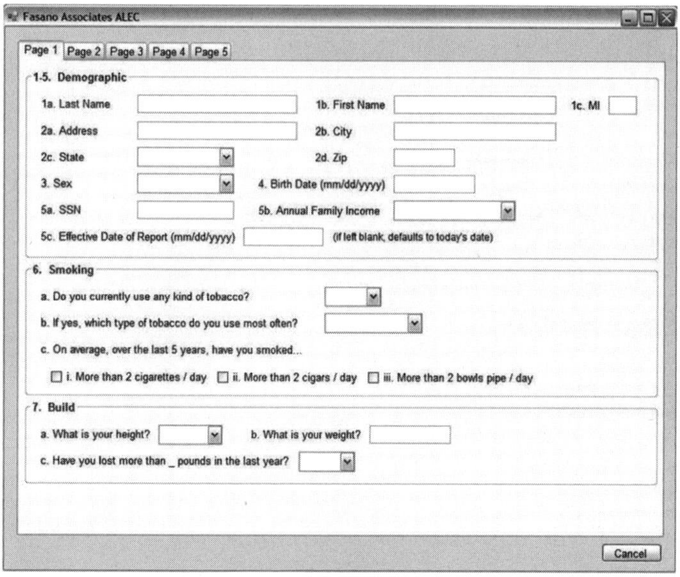

FIGURE 4.1 Fasano Online Calculator A
© Fasano Associates, Inc. December 2009.

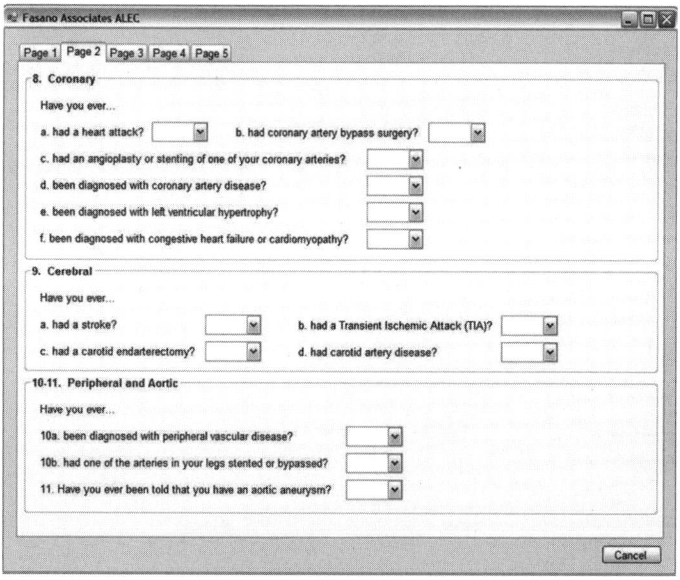

FIGURE 4.2 Fasano Online Calculator B
© Fasano Associates, Inc. December 2009.

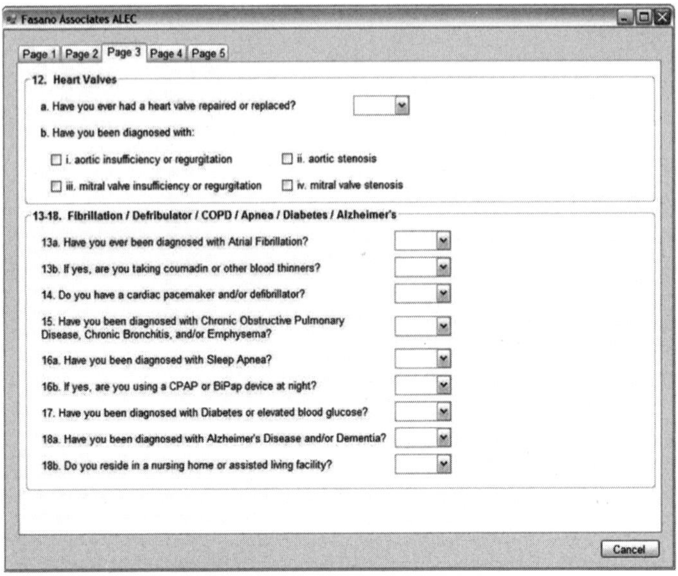

FIGURE 4.3   Fasano Online Calculator C
© Fasano Associates, Inc. December 2009.

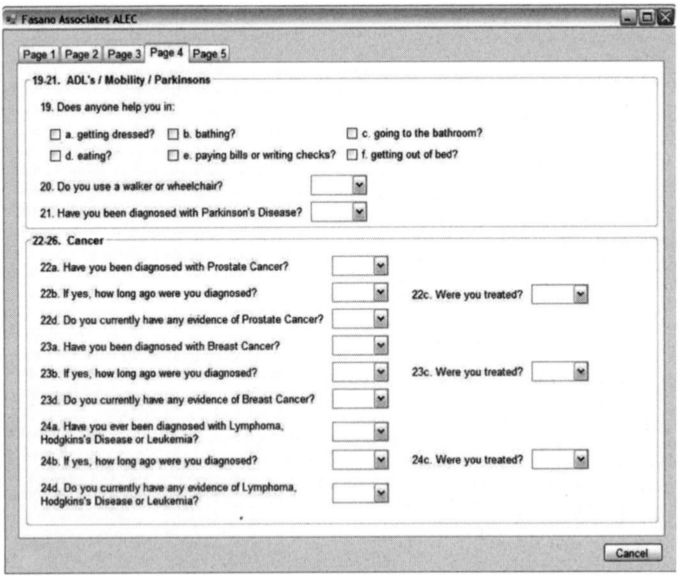

FIGURE 4.4   Fasano Online Calculator D
© Fasano Associates, Inc. December 2009.

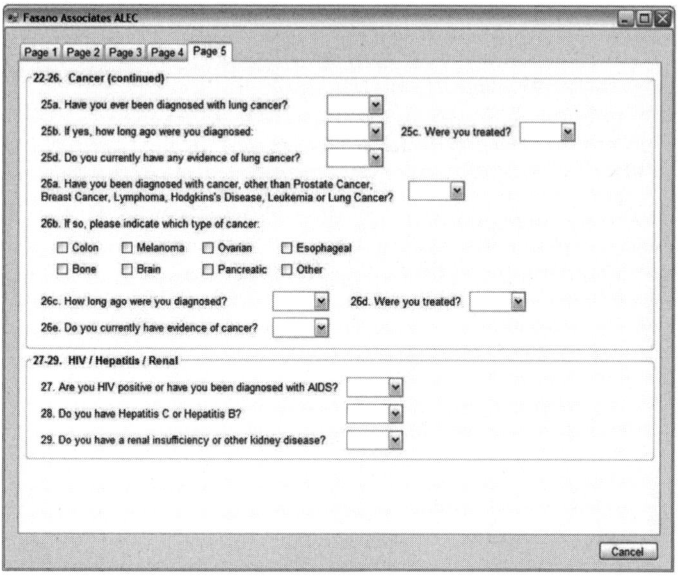

FIGURE 4.5 Fasano Online Calculator E
© Fasano Associates, Inc. December 2009.

It takes only a few minutes to fill out this simplified life expectancy calculator, yet it would allow the lender to improve the precision of its life expectancy estimating process and, in the process, be more responsive to the substantially untapped market for reverse mortgages.

BHUYAN'S FINAL POINTS

- As opposed to traditional home loans, reverse mortgages depend more on life expectancy than FICO scores.
- Reverse mortgage underwriting has not been developed similarly to the secondary market for life insurance.
- Improving the accuracy and efficiency of underwriting will result in a more efficient reverse mortgage market.
- Actuarial data on seniors, especially those over the age of 80, is still somewhat thin. Most actuarial tables rely on population data to fill in the gaps, which can be too general.

SUMMARY

Life expectancy is one of the most important variables in the reverse mortgage underwriting process. Yet, current underwriting practices are overly simplified to the point that they are limiting the size and the efficiency of the market. We have learned a great deal as to mortality patterns of the over-65 demographic, largely as a result of the underwriting expertise developed in the life settlement market. This experience should be used to improve reverse mortgage underwriting and thereby expand the market.

CHAPTER 5

Risk Mitigation from Existing and Proposed Financial Products

Nemo Perera

Managing Partner, Risk Capital Partners, LLC

Current trends in U.S. demographics suggest that the market for reverse mortgages will grow dramatically in the next decade as Baby Boomers cross into the qualifying age of 62. Given the recent challenges facing traditional mortgage originators from tighter credit and lending standards, reverse mortgages will see stronger interest from both lenders and investors (see Figure 5.1).

Growth can be attributed to the following primary drivers:

- The credit crisis and low-to-negative HPA (home price appreciation) has crippled origination volume and profitability in traditional mortgages.
- Baby Boomers,[1] the fastest growing cohort, have locked up vast amounts of home equity:
  - As of 2005, over 12 million senior households were free and clear of mortgage debt while only 12 thousand had reverse mortgages[2] (Figure 5.2).

    Over the next 5 years, 13 percent of the population will be 65 or older, and this cohort is expected to be 17.7 percent of the population by 2025 (Figure 5.3).

    Over 80MM people are due to start retiring in 2009.
- Reverse mortgages can provide essential financing to seniors as the public financial infrastructure erodes, as well as allow them to reside in comfort of their homes indefinitely.
  - The United States will not be able to grow its way out of long-term fiscal imbalances posed by rising health-care costs and the aging of

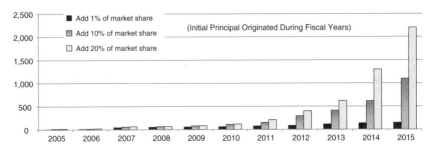

FIGURE 5.1 Reverse Mortgage Issuance Projections
Source: RBS Greenwich Capital, U.S. Census Bureau.

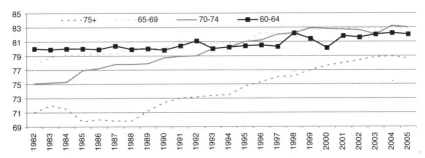

FIGURE 5.2 Homeownership Rates by Age Cohort
Source: RBS Greenwich Capital, U.S. Census Bureau.

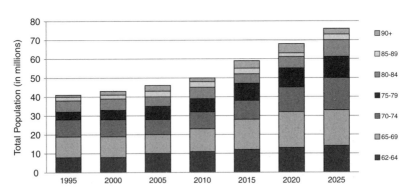

FIGURE 5.3 Projected U.S. Population Aged 62 and Over
Source: RBS Greenwich Capital, U.S. Census Bureau.

the population.[3] Bernanke urged Congress to begin tackling the problem right away and to set up milestones for progress.

- In July 2006, the U.S. House of Representatives passed legislation—Expanding Homeownership Act[4]—that would make substantial improvements to the Federal Housing Administration (FHA) reverse mortgage program. There is also proposed legislation by several states in recent years to limit Medicaid for individuals who have more than $500,000 in home equity.
- It has become more difficult for seniors to stay in their homes because of medical costs. The Center for Retirement Research asserts that 43 percent of working households were in danger of having too little income to fund their retirement needs.
- Moreover, there is a disincentive for seniors to sell their home because the equity proceeds render them ineligible for Medicaid.

Seniors can easily convert home equity to supplement retirement, pay medical and hospice costs, take vacations, and so forth, without tax events or any future payments. There is a real need for reverse mortgages as older Americans become a larger proportion of the population and spend more years living in retirement.

This is only one side of the equation; increases in supply and demand for the reverse mortgage product have been fueling growth. Reverse mortgages are particularly appealing to investors not only for the better spreads they offer relative to competing fixed income products, but also because they lack the primary risks inherent in traditional mortgages. The lower repayment or refinancing risk in reverse mortgages eliminates much of the uncertainty surrounding the timing of cash flows and the resulting negative convexity. Although borrowers are allowed to prepay the mortgage, the prepayment option is exercised less frequently.

- Seniors are less prone to refinance and optimize cash flows.
- The economics are usually poor (see Figure 5.4):
  - Typically the mortgage will grow faster than the value of the home, reducing any additional loan amount available as the mortgage seasons.
  - High transaction costs. Origination fees are 2 percent of the loan amount, and most reverse mortgages have adjustable rates that alleviate the need to refinance on a periodic basis when interest rates fall.

The resulting lack of interest rate sensitivity has further benefits for prospective investors: Reverse mortgages allow investors to diversify their

% Change in Mortgage Rate

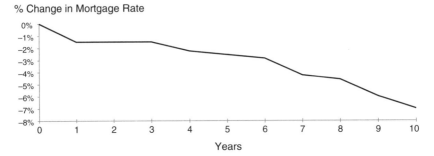

FIGURE 5.4 Breakeven Rate with 2 Percent Fee
Source: Lehman Brothers, *Introduction to Reverse Mortgage Securities.*

investments by reducing the covariance in their holdings, an important aspect in portfolio construction.

*   *   *

Another important point for today's investors given the recent surge in defaults for traditional mortgage, credit risk, and underwriting is de minimus; the underlying collateral is already owned by the borrower. Although credit and prepayment risks are not an issue, there are other risks that need to be identified and tailored to suit each investor's profile.

REVERSE MORTGAGE RISKS

Reverse mortgages have two distinct covenants:

1. The homeowner may stay in the property as long as the house is maintained and taxes are paid.
2. The lender has recourse only to the home; that is, reverse mortgages are nonrecourse and lenders have no lien on the estate of the homeowner or anything outside of the property.

The only two events that end the mortgage and allow the lender to take payment are mobility and mortality. Only death of the borrower (and coborrower in some cases), or a permanent displacement of the borrower through something such as a household move, can trigger a full payment. These rights for the borrower create risks unique to reverse mortgages because the borrower can keep the home indefinitely without additional payments while the loan continues to accrue interest. The primary risk for reverse mortgages is that the loan amount eventually exceeds (crosses over) the value of the property.

Components of Crossover Risk

The factors that shape the profile of crossover risk and reverse mortgage economics can be isolated and examined in further detail:

- *Home price risk:* If property values depreciate significantly, the crossover point will be reached sooner. Geographic concentration can also magnify this risk, as will loan seasoning, because the increase in the loan balance generally outpaces historic home price appreciation.
- *Interest rate risk:* An increase in interest rates increases the cost of funding in a securitization structure with floating rate bonds, whereas the increase in the interest rate for the collateral is effectively capped by the property value.
- *Actuarial risk:* Cash account loans have no stated maturity or term; therefore, borrowers who remain in their home for an extended period can cause crossover loss as the loan balance compounds every year going forward.

Figure 5.5 depicts how different home price appreciations can result in meaningful differences in crossover points.

A more competitive market from the sheer growth in reverse mortgage originators is better for the borrower, allowing for higher Loan-to-Value (LTV) loans today than in the past. Higher LTV rates increase the likelihood of crossover risk; but this risk is also being compounded by trends in

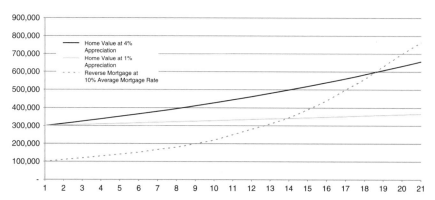

FIGURE 5.5 Crossover Points at Differing HPAs
Source: Lehman Brothers, Introduction to Reverse Mortgage Securities.

society, medical progress, and population. The elderly of today are living beyond projected life expectancies and staying in their homes significantly longer. Home hospice care is steadily replacing the nursing home option. Higher loan balances, longer life expectancies, and lower mobility are all factors that exacerbate crossover risk for reverse mortgage investors. At the outset of reverse mortgages in the 1980s, lenders mitigated such risk by lending relatively small amounts against the property, or through contingent interest[5] clauses, which allowed lenders to participate in home price appreciation by taking a stake in the equity in the home. However, the complete elimination of the contingent interest feature due to legal and moral hazard issues is another catalyst for the advent of structural and financial risk products. The ultimate investor of a non-agency reverse mortgage must manage risk through existing channels in the capital market or through new products that are emerging from the life industry.

AGENCY VERSUS NONCONFORMING LOANS

The majority of reverse mortgages are Home Equity Conversion Mortgages that are backed by the FHA (see Figures 5.6 and 5.7). Lenders originate to guidelines set by government agencies, and usually sell the loans to the agencies upon loan approval for a set profit. The economics are known and transparent for plain-vanilla originators.

Basic features are:

- One-year Constant Maturity Treasury Index (CMT) base index[6] + 2.0 percent gross margin, with 5 percent lifetime cap, plus a fixed servicing fee of $25 to $35 per month which is added to the loan balance.
- FHA insures three basic HECM products: *line of credit*, *term*, and *tenure*. Term and tenure receive a fixed monthly payment for stated time period (term) or for the life of the loan (tenure).

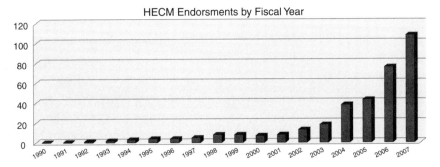

FIGURE 5.6 2005 Reverse Mortgage Market

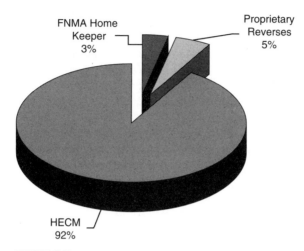

FIGURE 5.7 HECM Originations

- Loan size is capped. For HECMs, loan limit varies by area. Typical HECM might have average initial loan limit of $120,000, consisting of initial loan amount of $80,000 and available line of credit of $40,000.
- FHA charges both up-front and ongoing Mortgage Insurance Premium ("MIP"), equal to 2 percent of the Maximum Claim Amount at origination, plus 0.50 percent per annum on the unpaid balance during life of loan. When combined with lender's fees and other fees, total fees can approach $15,000.
- Lender fees are capped at greater of $2,000 and 2 percent of Maximum Claim Amount.

The HECM product is also an attractive investment vehicle for institutional investors who would hold the loans on their balance sheets or purchase them in the secondary market:

- The HECM product is credit risk free (in mortgage terms, the PO, principal-only, is safe):
  - The amount of the loans is significantly below the current market value for the house.
  - The loan is further discounted according to the age of the borrower.
  - Deals are backed by the FHA (with the full faith and credit of the U.S. government).
- The coupon is rich (in mortgage terms, the IO, interest-only, offers considerable yield) at CMT +1.50 percent (50-basis-point haircut for MIP).

Actuarial tables and mobility propensity will drive the prepayment option—not interest rates.

- Most importantly, a loan that has accreted to 98 percent of the available credit line can be put or assigned to Department of Housing and Urban Development (HUD). This option eliminates crossover risk and the associated losses from loan balances exceeding the value of the collateral.

Government National Mortgage Association (GNMA), also fully government sponsored, is currently in the early stages of wrapping loans and creating an agency program. The HECM *mortgage-backed security (MBS)* will allow approved issuers to securitize and sell their FHA loans in the form of a GNMA MBS.[7] This program will add additional transparency and liquidity, enhancing value for the end product.

Agency: FNMA

Federal National Mortgage Association (FNMA) was the original source of liquidity to originators that made HECM loans. Similar to its role in the forward market, FNMA paid originators a set price for all the conforming HECM loans brought to it.[8] Today, competing bids for HECMs from the likes of Wall Street banks have provided another outlet for originators, and better economics for originators and consumers as a result.

Additionally, in 1995, six years after the introduction of HECM, FNMA decided to take a more active role in reverse mortgages by offering the FNMA Home Keeper reverse mortgage.

There are two major differences between HECMs and the Home Keeper loans. First, the maximum claim amount can be larger because it is based on the conforming loan limit. Second, the reverse mortgage can be used for a home purchase, a feature not available to HECM borrowers.

Nonconforming Loans

Basic features are:

- LIBOR base index + higher margin.
- Higher limits on property value or loan size. (Average loan in SASCO 2006-RM1 equaled $335,268, secured by property value of $1,063,000.)
- Like HECM, jumbo borrower may initially borrow any percent of total loan amount available, based on the LTV ratio allowed for his or her age. The undrawn portion becomes the borrower's line of credit.
- Fees are typically smaller and can even be zero.

- Some jumbo loans have a feature that protects a portion of the borrower's equity. This feature allows the borrower to limit loan obligation to a stated percentage of the home's full market value, in exchange for the proportionately lower loan amount.

The percentage of nonconforming loans is less than 10 percent of the market. Since the introduction of HECM, the market share for non-agency loans has grown steadily every year. The prospects for even faster growth in this market stem from empirical trends and investor's needs:

- *For alternative interest rate structures beyond CMT:* LIBOR-based interest and fixed interest rate products.

  Lenders typically monetize loans through the securitization markets or sell wholesale packages of loans to banks, which are then usually securitized, for liquidity. Most securitizations are done with LIBOR or swapped into LIBOR because of investor profiles.
- *For larger loan amounts:* Many borrowers would exceed the current $417,000 lending limit imposed by HUD.[9] Larger loans, or *jumbo* loans, offer lines or payments of up to $10 million.
- *For more flexibility:* Borrowers are offered more options on access to their line of credit, and the availability of the proceeds.
- *For more availability:* There is also a proposal to lower the minimum age to 60, which would dramatically increase the lending base, adding the possibility of creating additional mortgage products.

  Reverse mortgages are exempt from Section 32 predatory lending laws. However, issuers would still have to contend with state regulatory hurdles.

Please see Table 5.1 for a comparison chart of the various RM products.

TABLE 5.1 Example Reverse Mortgage Market Products

Summary of Program Characteristics	Home Equity Conversion Mortgage (HECM)	Fannie Mae Home Keeper	Financial Freedom (Two Programs: Cash Account, Equity Guard)
Dates of operation	1989–present	1995–present	1993–present
Approximate market share	85%	10%	5%

(continued)

TABLE 5.1   (Continued)

Summary of Program Characteristics	Home Equity Conversion Mortgage (HECM)	Fannie Mae Home Keeper	Financial Freedom (Two Programs: Cash Account, Equity Guard)
Distribution	FHA-approved lenders in 49 states, D.C., and Puerto Rico	Fannie-Mae-approved lenders in 49 states and D.C.	Financial Freedom and correspondents in 12 states
Minimum borrow age	62	62	62
Eligible property limit	One-to-four-unit owner-occupied homes; FHA-approved manufactured homes; condominiums and planned unit developments	Single-family home or condominium; special product available for home purchase	Single-family home; one-to-four-unit dwellings; condominiums and planned unit developments
Payment options	Tenure; term; line of credit; modified tenure; modified term	Tenure; revolving line of credit; modified tenure	Lump sum; annuity; line of credit
Interest rate	Annual adjustable tied to one-year Treasury bill rate; annual has 2% annual and 5% lifetime caps; monthly has 10% lifetime cap; fixed rate possible but not used	Adjustable, based on weekly average of one-month secondary market CD index, with 12% lifetime cap	Cash Account: Semiannual adjustable tied to LIBOR. Equity Guard: no explicit interest rate; pure equity sharing arrangement
Origination fee	Greater of $2,000 or 2% of maximum claim amount	2% of home value or 2% of maximum lending value	2% of home value, maximum of $10,000
Insurance premium	2% of maximum claim amount at origination; 0.5% of outstanding balance (annual fee)	1% origination fee; no explicit premium but all interest payments to Fannie Mae	None

Insurance	Lender may assign mortgage to FHA when loan reaches 98% of home value	"Self-insured" by FNMA	None
Servicing fees	Maximum $30/ month for fixed rate or annual adjustable; $35 for monthly adjustable	Between $15/ month and $30/ month	Cash Account: $20/month Equity Guard: None
Servicing	FHA-approved servicers	Fannie Mae– approved servicers	Financial Freedom

Source: Lehman Brothers, "Evaluation Report of FHA's Home Equity Conversion Mortgage Insurance Demonstration."

SUMMARY

The major risk for reverse mortgages, crossover risk, is eliminated for the majority of reverse mortgage loans because of the government-sponsored-agency programs.

Now that causes of this risk have been identified, Chapter 6 deals with products and programs designed to mitigate risk for reverse mortgages that do not fall under the agency guarantees.

BHUYAN'S FINAL POINTS

■ Although government agencies bear the risks associated with conforming reverse mortgages for lenders, this inherently caps the growth of the market to what the government is willing to absorb in losses. This is especially so because 90 percent of reverse mortgages are agency backed.

■ The ballooning U.S. balance sheet will also reduce the confidence that lenders have in U.S.-backed assets that may be originated inefficiently.

■ Agency reverse mortgages rely on outdated actuarial data as their motives are not profit based.

■ Nonconforming reverse mortgages present an opportunity for lenders to issue lower-risk and more profitable reverse mortgage loans.

NOTES

1. Population born between 1946–1964.
2. 2005 HUD Census Section 7-15.
3. Fed Chairman Testimony, January 18, 2007.
4. H.R. 5121.
5. Contingent interest loans require the borrower to pay a share of the underlying property appreciation or value in addition to principal and accrued interest. In exchange, the borrower receives significantly higher loan proceeds. No contingent interest loan has been originated for several years. Appreciation share loans are permitted under the HECM program, and at one time comprised a majority of the jumbo market.
6. The One-Year Constant Maturity Treasury Rate is made available from the Federal Reserve Board. The index is derived from the average yield on U.S. Treasury securities adjusted to a constant maturity of one year, interpolated from the U.S. daily yield curve, which relates the yield on a security to its time to maturity.
7. GNMA press release, October 17, 2006; www.ginniemae.gov.
8. FNMA's set price was 102 for HECM, which means that the agency would pay 102 percent of the loan made. The economics for the originator before costs was 2 percent of the mortgage face value.
9. The economic stimulation bill signed by President Obama raised the national loan limit for HECM loans to 150 percent of FHLMC loan limits criteria, or $625,500. However, this higher loan limit was available only for the balance of the year in 2009.

CHAPTER 6

Longevity Risk and Fair Value Accounting

Peter M. Mazonas, CPA
Life Settlement Financial, LLC

The technical parts of this chapter are extracted from testimony given by this author on November 2, 2009, before the Securities and Exchange Commission's Life Settlement Task Force. The original copywrited documents are available at www.LifeSettlementFinancial.com.

Reverse mortgages and life settlements are sister asset classes. Both reverse mortgages and life settlements are longevity-dependent assets, where the value and thus initial pricing is dependent on an unobservable future event—the death of the borrower or the insured. This chapter investigates and demonstrates a better way of predicting life expectancy, *moveout*, for an individual reverse mortgage loan. The methodology described can be easily built into the loan origination process with significant advantages to both senior borrowers, while affording investors and the American taxpayers more accurate individual loan pricing, portfolio valuation, and transparency.

There has been little incentive to reevaluate and then alter the pricing components of the existing Home Equity Conversion Mortgage (HECM) reverse mortgage. These Federal Housing Administration (FHA) loans are offered by mortgage brokers, backed by a Ginnie Mae guarantee, and securitized by large institutions.

Reexamination of reverse mortgage moveout determination is important today as regulators, rating agencies, and the accounting profession meet the requirements of fair value accounting. Every securitized portfolio of reverse mortgages that is issued as a security, or where investors in the portfolio issue audited financial statements, will have to annually comply with fair value accounting. Specific methodologies to revalue each loan in the portfolio and mark the portfolio to market are defined by the Financial Accounting Standards Board (FASB) and the International Accounting Standards Board (IASB).

Basing moveout on values derived from large-population mortality tables that have been known for 30 years to be flawed[1] creates significant liability for bankers selling the securities, auditors and actuaries who attest to portfolio valuations, and the lawyers structuring the transactions.

Proper reverse mortgage design requires an accurate understanding and prediction of the three main variables used to price each loan:

1. Appraised home value at origination.
2. Interest rate risk, especially for variable rate loans.
3. An accurate assessment of loan term based on the non-institutionalized life expectancy of the borrower, or the survivor in the case of a couple.

Historically, the estimated loan term, typically called "moveout," for a reverse mortgage has been determined using large-population mortality tables, typically the Social Security Administration Mortality Tables. These are derived from the U.S. Decennial Life Tables (USDLT), published every 10 years. By definition, *average life expectancy (LE)* is that point in the future when 50 percent of a large population will have died and 50 percent will still be alive. The use of these tables simplified the determination of the term for each loan to a table lookup and added uniformity to product design.

For each loan to be accurately priced, and thus a portfolio to be accurately valued, two longevity factors are critical:

1. The applicability and accuracy of the methodology for determining morbidity (onset of sickness) and mortality (death).
2. Determination of the future point in time when morbidity will force the senior to move out because of his or her need for institutional care, thus terminating the loan.

A number of problems exist in using large-population mortality tables to define the term of each loan. This easy solution has been a disservice both to senior borrowers and to investors who purchase interest in securitized pools of reverse mortgages. Using average life expectancy to predict the loan term means that half of the borrowers will live longer than the average. Someone or something has to pay for this risk if the product design is going to be valid and yield the expected rate of return. Early product designers hedged their bet and balanced the *who* and *what* that would compensate for error in product design and execution. Loan payments to borrowers were reduced so the "underpayments" to the 50 percent who died early or on time offset the extra payments made to the long-lived borrowers. The *what* was requiring borrowers to make an upfront mortgage insurance premium payment mandatory from their first loan part of the popular HUD/FHA Home Equity Conversion Mortgage (HECM). It was anticipated that this would solve the longevity risk element of product design.

Controlling longevity risk in this way has now been shown to no longer work. The 2 percent mortgage insurance premium charged at origination on each loan and added to a risk premium pool has proven to be inadequate to cover the combination of longevity risk and interest rate risk. For HECM loans, when the principal is paid out, and the accumulated accrued interest equals the maximum loan amount, each loan is "put" back to FHA under the Ginnie Mae guarantee. To the extent losses exceed the value of the mortgage insurance pool, the American taxpayers absorb the loss with more national debt.

This shortcoming or design flaw was anticipated by product designers, including this author, who designed and patented Transamerica Home-First's lifetime reverse mortgage, "HouseMoney." Using outside actuarial consultants, HomeFirst relied on new data gathered from the National Long Term Care Survey (NLTCS). In 1984, the U.S. government, as part of the new Medicare program, began gathering assessment data on more than 32,000 seniors between the ages of 65 and 69. More specific data was gathered by Cologne Reinsurance on seniors in assisted living and skilled nursing facilities across the country.

The Cologne Re data was interpreted by actuary Phillip Barckman. By 1989, Barckman was convinced there was a correlation between an individual's loss of *activities of daily living (ADLs)* and the need for institutional care. With some exceptions, most seniors would like to age in place in their home and familiar surroundings. Based on observation of data, Barackman hypothesized that at the loss of two ADLs a senior would be able to remain non-institutionalized only with the help of a cohort. By the time he or she lost three ADLs, the senior would require institutional care or in-home health care. Look at the following list and imagine your condition having lost two and then three of these capabilities:

- Personal hygiene
- Dressing and undressing
- Eating
- Transferring from bed to chair and back
- Voluntary bladder/bowel control
- Elimination
- Moving around (as opposed to being bedridden)

Approximately the first 1,000 lifetime reverse mortgages written by Transamerica HomeFirst from 1993 through 1994 based moveout on large-population age-based statistical data that extrapolated when the borrower would have lost 2.5 ADLs. Moveout for each loan pricing was at that point. Actuaries from Ernst & Young, Transamerica's auditors, objected to this methodology and forced HomeFirst to conform to conventional wisdom and use Social Security mortality table data to estimate a borrower's moveout.

In 1980 and 1981, a design committee created an individual-level assessment tool for the Social Security Administration that collected medical, activity of daily living (ADL), instrumental activity of daily living (IADL), cognitive, and other sociodemographic/behavioral variables. A subset of these questions was developed into a questionnaire assessment tool for the Center for Medicare and Medicaid Services (CMS). CMS later started requiring quarterly assessments of Medicare recipient residents in assisted-living and skilled nursing facilities. One company that developed a computer-based version of this assessment tool similar to the questionnaire developed for the NLTCS was Vigilan Systems, in Wilsonville, Oregon. Individual resident–level data gathered using the Vigilan *Administrator* assessment tool has subsequently confirmed Barckman's hypothesis of when seniors move from their homes.[2] Vigilan data shows that the average resident stays in assisted living for 25 months, after which he or she moves out because of increased morbidity or death.

Longevity-valued assets (LVA), specifically reverse mortgages and life settlements, are today being mispriced because (1) the reference tables being used to predict the insured's life expectancy for pricing are population- or subpopulation-based tables and (2) the multiplicative rating factors applied to those tables are biased. Understanding the origins and workings of these reference tables is important to understanding their flaws.

The force of mortality exhibits exponential growth above about age 20. This was discovered by Gompertz (1825), who published the famous "law of mortality" that now bears his name.[3] The Gompertz law can be written with three elements: (1) a continuous exponential function of age, (2) with a growth constant, and (3) a proportionality constant (details given in the following).[4]

The Gompertz law has been evaluated in numerous studies.[5] Several problems have been identified. (1) The fitted Gompertz function tends to overestimate mortality above about 80–90 years of age. (2) The Gompertz "constants" are not really constant; they differ from one population to another and over calendar time and cohort within a given population.[6] (3) The numerical values of two of the constants are negatively correlated when calculated for populations with a broad range of mortality conditions.[7]

Despite these problems, the Gompertz function provides a useful approximation to the age-specific mortality probabilities and an even better approximation to the age-specific mortality "hazard rates." The typical annual increase in age-specific mortality is in the range of 8–10 percent per year. All Gompertz functions are proportional to each other. Using the rule of 72, this implies a doubling time of 7.2–9 years of individual mortality probability. If the doubling times for individual mortality probability are constant in the range of 7.2–9 years, then it is reasonable to infer the underlying function is Gompertz. If doubling time is not constant, then the mortality is non-Gompertz (Figure 6.1). This means the exponential tables use a constant multiplier to increase the probability of death at increased age irrespective of the individual's personal characteristics.

The problem with the multiplicative model is that individual mortality does not appear to follow the Gompertz function, even approximately.[8] If mortality is not proportional to Gompertz, then the multiplicative model is incorrect and should not be relied on. The Social Security, USDLT, and other exponential large-population mortality tables are Gompertz.

In 2007, the *North American Actuarial Journal*, after two years of peer review, published a paper by P. J. Eric Stallard, Associate Director, Center for Population Health and Aging, Duke University, entitled *Trajectories of Morbidity, Disability, and Mortality Among the U.S. Elderly Population: Evidence from the 1984–1999 NLTCS.*[9] Unlike medical records' only mortality-predictive tools based on large-population reference tables, Stallard's model describes health and the probability of death at the individual level without assuming any specific functional form for the increase of mortality over age or of the ratios of mortality between individuals and the population to which they belong (e.g., non-Gompertz). Stallard is the 2006 recipient of the Edward A. Lew award from the American Society of Actuaries for his work in longevity-specific actuarial modeling.

The results of that analysis were surprising and illuminating. The rates of increase in the mortality probabilities for individuals were both faster and slower than the average rate of increase in the study population, with the slowest rates of increase occurring at the highest mortality levels and the fastest rates at the lowest mortality levels. However, there was substantial heterogeneity in the rates of increase at the lowest mortality levels, making it difficult to generalize the pattern of increase for individuals without considering their individual risk profiles.

Simplistically but true, unhealthy people die at a faster rate and healthy people die at a slower rate. Ask any nurse in a senior care community and he or she will tell you that much about the mortality curve of an individual is not contained in their medical records.

Life Settlement Financial owns the commercial rights to this model, now named Longevity Cost Calculator™ (LCC).[10] The LCC model clearly shows that impairments in *activities of daily living (ADLs)*, *instrumental activities of daily living (IADLs)*, range of motion, and cognition are greater predictors of morbidity and mortality than are individual or groups of medical conditions or table values. The LCC is the only current predictive model to scientifically do this.

Unlike large-population-based mortality tables, the LCC uses a questionnaire assessment model to evaluate the overall health of individuals and predict the degradation of their health. This allows the model to distinguish between when the senior is able to live in the community independently and when he or she must move out permanently to receive institutional care.

Using linear regression analysis, the actual-versus-expected accuracy of the Longevity Cost Calculator™ model is validated at 96 percent or greater. This mortality accuracy also applies to the important prediction of how long an individual will remain living in the community before he or she should move out to an institutional setting. This means that the predicted year-over-year annual mortality has this degree of accuracy. It is interesting to note that when the above 95 predictor variables are Chi-square ranked, not until number 26 of 95 do you find a variable typically found on medical records.[11]

This model has been in use by the Centers for Medicare and Medicaid Services (CMS) and the National Council on the Aging for three years as the Long-Term Care Planning Tool on the Medicare web site. For documentation of the methodology, see www.medicare.gov. The mortality model has since been independently implemented in the Longevity Cost Calculator and a working web-based model is available at www.lifesettlement financial.com.

In addition to proper longevity valuation at the individual loan and portfolio levels, the size of pooled loan portfolios is also important and often misunderstood by investors. Assuming there has been consistent and proper loan underwriting, not until a portfolio contains at least 384 loans can one expect to have an accuracy of +/-10.0 percent at a 95 percent probability level.[12] Not until at least 1,537 loans can you expect an accuracy of +/-5.0 percent at the same 95 percent probability level.[13] This means that at a minimum, a reverse mortgage loan portfolio must contain $100 million of loans. A more appropriate portfolio size would be in excess of $400 million of loan amount. This dollar size is the reason I assert that these portfolios, now or during their life, will be audited under GAAP and may be under the oversight of the Public Company Accounting Oversight Board (PCAOB) because issuers of audited financial statements are holding these portfolios as investments. At the PCAOB's Standing Advisory Group

Meeting on October 14–15, 2009, staff called for a standards-setting project to revise its existing standards on auditing fair value measurement.[14]

LONGEVITY COST CALCULATOR™ AS A LOAN UNDERWRITING AND PRICING TOOL

The completed Longevity Cost Calculator™ questionnaire, in addition to providing an LE and moveout date, scores each insured using a four-level Grade of Measurement (GoM) system. As per the earlier-referenced material on the Life Settlement Financial web site, the interrelationship of an insured's ADLs, IADLs and possible cognitive impairment affects those GoM scores and the trajectory of the individual's survival curve is used to price a settlement offer. To facilitate the description of the health changes, the model generates time-invariant GoM scores that characterize the predicted health status of each person at the time he or she is/was in the youngest age group in the calibration dataset, which for the current implementation is age group 65–69.

GoM 1 (also referred to as "Pure Type I" or "Type I," with Roman numerals designating the rank ordering of the states by health status; we use the shorter GoM 1–4 reference throughout this document) refers to the healthiest component of the population. GoM scores 2–4 capture a range of health problems that occur at different ages, with progressive and graded transitions from GoM 2 to GoM 3 and 4. GoM 2 scores refer to people who have numerous medical problems, but few if any ADL or other functional problems, or cognitive impairment. Persons with initial strong scores (i.e., close to 1.0, or 100%) on GoM 2 will live longer than traditional LE providers estimate; although this changes at older ages where these persons transition to strong scores on GoM 4. Persons with strong scores on GoM 3 have minor medical problems, but mild/moderate cognitive impairments, usually not indicated in their medical records, although this also changes at older ages where these persons transition to strong scores on GoM 4. Strong scores on GoM 4 identify people who have more serious medical problems, combined with serious ADL and/or cognitive impairments, usually not indicated in their medical records. People with initial strong scores on GoM 3 and GoM 4 will have shorter LEs than those issued by traditional LE underwriters.

Recall that the LE is the area under the relevant survival curve for the person or population for which the LE is being calculated. Thus, differences in LE between persons or groups of persons are best understood by examining the associated survival curves. This is illustrated in the graph in Figure 6.1, which plots the survival curves for males assessed at age 82 (i.e., age at

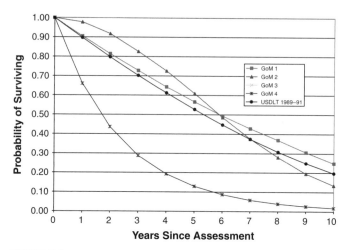

FIGURE 6.1   Probability of Surviving for Each of 10 Years Following
Initial Assessment at Age 82, Males, by Initial Time-Invariant GoM Pure
Type and for the U.S. Decennial Life Table for 1989–1991

last birthday is 82) for the next 10 years following the assessment, with a
separate curve shown for each of the four time-invariant GoM pure types,
and also for comparison the survival curve from the U.S. Decennial Life
Table (USDLT) for 1989–1991.

According to the USDLT, the male LE at age 82 is 6.2 years. This value
is less than the LEs of 6.9 and 6.3 years for GoM 1 and 2, but is substantially higher than the LEs of 2.5 years each for GoM 3 and 4 (the values are
the same because an initial GoM 3 "converts" to GoM 4 prior to age 82).

Importantly, given that both the survival curve and its slope are used to
price a loan (the former to determine the duration of loan payments,
the latter for loan maturity offsets), it is important to accurately estimate
these quantities.

On the graph in Figure 6.1, you will note that an initial GoM 2 has approximately a 16 percent greater likelihood of surviving through years 1
through 5 until the lines converge at year 6, near the 6.2-year LE. On the other
hand, an initial GoM 3 or 4 has approximately a 75 percent lower likelihood
of surviving through years 1 through 5, with corresponding reductions for
persons who have initial *fractional* scores on GoM 3 or 4, with complementary *fractional* scores on GoM 1 and/or 2. The sum of all fractional scores
must equal 1.0 (100%), with the scores for any given individual derived from
his or her answers to the 76 questions on the application form.

The corresponding graph (Figure 6.2) for females aged 82 years at
assessment displays similar patterns, but with a somewhat longer LE, 7.8

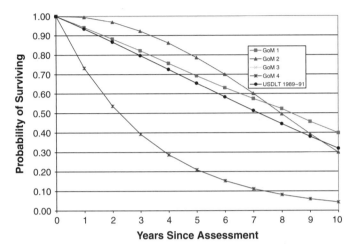

FIGURE 6.2 Probability of Surviving for Each of 10 Years Following Initial Assessment at Age 82, Females, by Initial Time-Invariant GoM Pure Type and for the U.S. Decennial Life Table for 1989–1991

years in the USDLT, which is less than the LEs of 9.2 and 8.2 years for GoM 1 and 2, but is substantially higher than the LEs of 3.2 years each for GoM 3 and 4 (as for males, the values are the same because an initial GoM 3 "converts" to GoM 4 prior to age 82).

For both sexes, the differences in the survival curves and their slopes illustrate the potential for substantial mispricing without this additional knowledge concerning the level and slope of the relevant survival curves. Individual-moveout-level pricing would correct this problem and accurately match loan payments to the senior's anticipated tenure in his or her home.

Longevity Cost Calculator: Actual versus Expected Accuracy

The Longevity Cost Calculator™ web-based model is a validated replication of the original peer-reviewed model published in the *North American Actuarial Journal*. The original model was calibrated using 120,832 male person-years of consecutive assessment data and 196,270 female person-years over an 18-year period commencing with the 1984 National Long Term Care Survey. The annual mortality probabilities were based on 20,428 deaths (8,583 males and 11,845 females) among 32,389 participants in the survey (12,974 males and 19,415 females) in the 18-year period.

Shown here are a table (Table 6.1) and two graphs (Figures 6.3 and 6.4) reproduced from the 2007 *NAAJ* paper. Table 6.1 shows the predicted

TABLE 6.1 Probabilities of Death within One Year in Four Pure Types of GoM Models, Adjusted for Declines in Vitality, by Sex and Attained Age at Time of Exposure

Exposure Age	Number of Person-Years at Risk[a]	Annual Probability by Type				Observed Probability	Predicted Probability
		I	II	III	IV		
Males							
65–69	20,323	0.000	0.000	0.132	0.138	0.031	0.032
70–74	38,255	0.002	0.005	0.194	0.246	0.043	0.044
75–79	31,291	0.038	0.013	0.319	0.319	0.067	0.067
80–84	19,170	0.095	0.023	0.340	0.340	0.105	0.106
85–89	8,117	0.127	0.202	0.330	0.330	0.154	0.155
90–94	2,728	0.198	0.323	0.323	0.032	0.228	0.229
95–99	793	0.226	0.434	0.434	0.434	0.301	0.301
100–104	155	0.372	0.528	0.528	0.528	0.400	0.401
Total	120,832	0.041	0.033	0.253	0.271	0.071	0.072
Females							
65–69	25,424	0.000	0.000	0.081	0.140	0.017	0.017
70–74	52,008	0.001	0.003	0.108	0.223	0.027	0.003
75–79	48,498	0.018	0.003	0.249	0.249	0.043	0.043
80–84	35,563	0.059	0.005	0.267	0.267	0.070	0.070
85–89	20,404	0.089	0.110	0.271	0.271	0.115	0.115
90–94	9,577	0.127	0.272	0.272	0.272	0.183	0.184
95–99	3,804	0.168	0.388	0.388	0.388	0.264	0.264
100–104	992	0.274	0.499	0.499	0.499	0.325	0.324
Total	196,270	0.036	0.037	0.201	0.239	0.060	0.061

[a]Includes up to four observations per respondent; excludes respondents age 65–69 in 1999.
Source: Author's calculations based on data from the NLTCS.

probability of death within each year contrasted to the observed death of individuals in the assessment population. These are shown in age brackets by the 5-year age groups (age at start of each 1-year follow-up) used for model estimation as well as the total over age of the observed-versus-predicted mortality for males and females.

The differences between the observed and predicted age-specific death probabilities are very small and are statistically nonsignificant, with chi-squared values of 1.36 and 0.29, respectively, each with 6 degrees of freedom (d.f.) (reference values are 12.59 and 16.81 at the conventional 5%

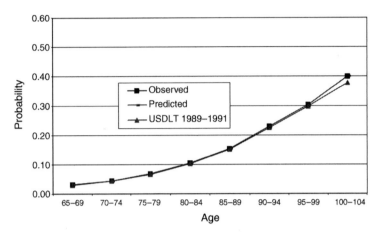

FIGURE 6.3 Probability of Death within One Year, Males

and 1% significance levels). The graphs show the same data but add the corresponding death probabilities from the U.S. Decennial Life Table (USDLT) for 1989–1991.

In the following, we attempt to translate these values into the numbers presented by commercial LE providers who represent that they are accurate 86 to 96 percent of the time. They do not provide or publish the basis for their estimates. Hence, we cannot be certain that our measures of accuracy are fully comparable with theirs.

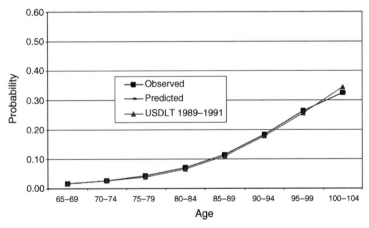

FIGURE 6.4 Probability of Death within One Year, Females

TABLE 6.2 Credibility and Event Counts

Maximum Acceptable Departure from the Expected Count	Probability of Observed Count Falling within the Acceptable Range		
	90%	95%	99%
	Minimum Required Expected Count		
+/−2.5%	4,329	6,146	**10,616**
+/−5.0%	**1,082**	1,537	2,654
+/−7.5%	481	683	1,180
+/−10%	271	384	663
+/−20%	68	**96**	166
+/−30%	30	43	74
+/−40%	17	24	41
+/−50%	**11**	15	27

Source: Based on Longley-Cook (1962).

To begin consideration of measures of accuracy, it is useful to consider the random statistical fluctuations that are expected from estimates based on the different numbers of events likely to be observed in different-sized samples, assuming fixed underlying event rates. Table 6.2 shows the minimum number of expected events needed to cap the maximum relative error (e.g., [observed number of deaths minus expected number of deaths] ÷ [expected number of deaths]) with one of three levels of confidence.

To be 99 percent confident that the maximum relative error is less than 2.5 percent, the sample size needs to be large enough to produce 10,616 deaths (in bold in the table). The annual mortality probabilities in the *NAAJ* analysis were based on 20,428 deaths (8,583 males and 11,845 females), indicating that the total rates are very stable but the stratifications by age and other variables may be affected by random statistical fluctuations. To be 90 percent confident that the maximum relative error is less than 5 percent, the sample size needs to be large enough to produce 1,082 deaths, which is the standard size used for full credibility in the actuarial literature. To be 95 percent confident that the maximum relative error is less than 20 percent, the sample size needs to be large enough to produce 96 deaths, which rounds to about 100. To be 90 percent confident that the maximum relative error is less than 50 percent, the sample size needs to be large enough to produce 11 deaths, which rounds to about 10. Thus, as the expected number of deaths falls from 10,000 to 1,000 to 100 to 10, the relative error increases from about 2.5 to 50 percent.

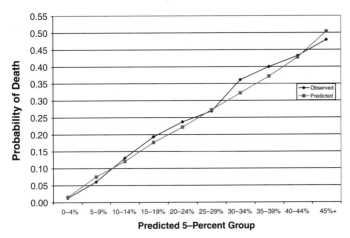

FIGURE 6.5 Observed and Predicted Probabilities of Death, Males, by Predicted-Probability Class Intervals with Cutpoints at Multiples of 5 Percent

Practical considerations often dictate sample sizes less than that needed for full actuarial credibility. Table 6.2 indicates that sample sizes of 271 and 384 can yield relative errors of ±10 percent at the 90 and 95 percent confidence levels, respectively.

Random statistical fluctuations are inherently unpredictable. Hence, our measures of accuracy must focus on our ability to generate accurate values for the expected number of deaths among any selected set of insured lives.

The tables and graphs from the *NAAJ* paper (Table 6.1; Figures 6.3 and 6.4) show that this can be done for groups of insured lives when the groups are defined on the basis of age and sex.

The next two graphs (Figures 6.5 and 6.6) show the performance of the model when the NLTCS mortality-exposure data is grouped into 10 categories according to the predicted probability of death, based on the use of fixed cutpoints at multiples of .05 (5%), separately for males and females. Chi-squared statistical tests of fit of the models are presented separately in Tables 6.3 and 6.4.

Visually, one can see that the observed probabilities increase across the 10 categories for both sexes, except for category 9 for females. However, the chi-square test of the deviation for that one point indicates that the difference is statistically nonsignificant, with a chi-squared value of 3.44 with 1 d.f. (Table 6.4; reference values are 3.84 and 6.63 at the conventional 5% and 1% significance levels).

The Hosmer-Lemeshow chi-squared test produces statistically significant total chi-squared values of 155.65 and 62.99, respectively, for males

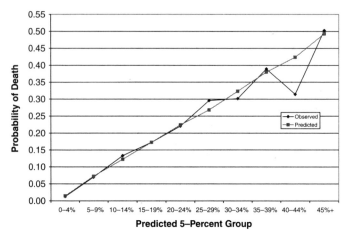

FIGURE 6.6 Observed and Predicted Probabilites of Death, Females, by Predicted-Probability Class Intervals with Cutpoints at Multiples of 5 Percent

and females, each with 8 d.f. (reference values are 15.51 and 20.09 at the conventional 5% and 1% significance levels).

Several comments are in order:

1. The tests indicate that the models displayed in Figures 6.5 and 6.6 do *not* fit the data. This means that at least some of the deviations of the observed from predicted numbers of deaths are larger than expected by chance.

TABLE 6.3 Observed and Predicted Probability of Death, Males, by Predicted-Probability Class Intervals with Cutpoints at Multiples of 5 Percent

Percentage Group	Number of Person-Years at Risk	Observed Number of Deaths	Expected Number of Deaths	Observed Probability	Predicted Probability	Hosmer-Lemeshow Chi-Squared
0–4%	61,463	801	981	0.013	0.016	33.60
5–9%	23,256	1,407	1,747	0.061	0.075	71.73
10–14%	20,100	2,622	2,420	0.130	0.120	19.20
15–19%	7,705	1,490	1,363	0.193	0.177	14.29
20–24%	4,557	1,082	1,011	0.237	0.222	6.44
25–29%	2,095	563	571	0.269	0.273	0.16
30–34%	1,361	492	438	0.361	0.322	9.73
35–39%	115	46	43	0.400	0.372	0.04
40–44%	132	57	56	0.432	0.428	0.01
45%+	48	23	24	0.479	0.504	0.11
Total	120,832	8,583	8,655	0.071	0.072	155.65

TABLE 6.4 Observed and Predicted Probability of Death, Females, by Predicted-Probability Class Intervals with Cutpoints at Multiples of 5 Percent

Percentage Group	Number of Person-Years at Risk	Observed Number of Deaths	Expected Number of Deaths	Observed Probability	Predicted Probability	Hosmer-Lemeshow Chi-Squared
0–4%	111,425	1,434	1,614	0.013	0.014	**20.33**
5–9%	44,837	3,124	3,239	0.070	0.072	4.42
10–14%	18,004	2,396	2,202	0.133	0.122	**19.46**
15–19%	10,245	1,770	1,770	0.173	0.173	0.00
20–24%	6,536	1,443	1,465	0.221	0.224	0.43
25–29%	3,413	1,009	915	0.296	0.268	**13.17**
30–34%	617	186	199	0.301	0.323	1.32
35–39%	914	356	347	0.389	0.380	0.35
40–44%	70	22	30	0.314	0.424	3.44
45%+	209	105	103	0.502	0.493	0.08
Total	196,270	11,845	11,885	0.060	0.061	**62.99**

2. These are identified by the boldface font in the rightmost columns of Tables 6.3 and 6.4 using a cutpoint equal to the critical value of 6.63 using the conventional 1 percent significance level.

3. For males, the five significant deviations are for the four lowest probability groups 0–19 percent and 30–34 percent; for females, the three significant deviations are for the 0–4 percent, 10–14 percent, and 25–29 percent probability groups.

4. The expected counts for the eight groups with significant deviations ranged from 438 to 2,420, and five of the eight exceed the 1,082 cutpoint for highly credible data in Table 6.2.

We conclude that there are factors operating in these data that are not represented in our model. This should not be surprising given that our model uses four GoM scores to summarize data on the full set of 76 questions concerning medical conditions, activities of daily living (ADLs), and cognitive and behavioral impairments. Moreover, there may be other influential factors not included in our set of 76 questions. Given a sufficiently large sample, one would expect to identify significant deviations from *any model* using the statistical procedures described previously.

Two additional comments provide additional perspective:

1. Only two groups had significant deviations for both sexes: the 0–4 percent and 10–14 percent probability groups. This suggests that the deviations from the models are not predictable.

2. Nonrandom deviations in the LCC models can be tolerated if they are sufficiently small, relative to the errors that would occur in the absence of the LCC models.

To quantify the size of the nonrandom deviations, Stallard applied linear regression analysis with the observed probabilities regressed on the predicted probabilities, as shown in Tables 6.3 and 6.4, obtaining R-squared values of 0.985 and 0.942, respectively.

The average of these two R-squared values is 0.964, which may be interpreted as a measure of the accuracy of the LCC models: 96.4 percent of the variance of the observed probabilities is accounted for by the expected probabilities produced by the LCC models. The remaining 3.6 percent of the variance constitutes a tolerable level of nonrandom deviations in the LCC models.

We considered the possibility that the linear regression analysis may not fully represent the impact of small deviations at the lower probability levels in Tables 6.3 and 6.4. This was motivated in part by the chi-squared tests, which indicated that most of these deviations were statistically significant. To deal with this issue, we generated a second set of regressions with the logarithms of the observed probabilities regressed on the logarithms of the predicted probabilities, obtaining R-squared values of 0.994 and 0.989, respectively.

The average of these two R-squared values is 0.991, which may be interpreted as an alternative measure of the accuracy of the LCC models: 99.1 percent of the variance of the logarithm of the observed probabilities is accounted for by the logarithm of the expected probabilities produced by the LCC models. The remaining 0.9 percent of the variance constitutes an even more tolerable level of nonrandom deviations in the LCC models.

Two additional questions are important to our assessment of the accuracy of the model.

The first question is whether the GoM scores add any significant information beyond the information already available using the age-specific mortality probabilities displayed in Figures 6.3 and 6.4, and if so, how much? This question can be directly addressed using the log–likelihood-ratios for the four sex-specific models listed in Table 6.5 to generate the corresponding AIC (Akaike Information Criterion) and BIC (Bayesian Information Criterion) statistics typically used for model assessment.

Model 1 is the simplest model. It assumes that the sex-specific mortality probability is constant over age and GoM scores. Model 2 assumes that the sex-specific mortality probabilities increase over age but not over GoM scores, following the observed values displayed in Figures 6.3 and 6.4. Model 3 assumes that the sex-specific mortality probabilities increase over

TABLE 6.5 Log-Likelihood-Ratios for Four Sex-Specific Models with Corresponding AIC and BIC Statistics Used for Model Assessment

# Model Description	Log-Likelihood-Ratio	d.f.	AIC	BIC	ΔAIC	ΔBIC
Males						
1. Constant Probability	0.00	1	2.00	9.06	10,878.66	10,659.87
2. Age-Specific Probability (no GoM)	1,632.10	8	−3,248.19	−3,191.73	7,628.46	7,459.08
3. GoM-Specific Probabilities (no Age)	5,278.87	4	−10,549.75	−10,521.52	326.91	129.30
4. Age & GoM-Specific Probabilities	5,470.33	32	−10,876.66	−10,650.82	0.00	0.00
Females						
1. Constant Probability	0.00	1	2.00	9.38	16,276.04	16,047.27
2. Age-Specific Probability (no GoM)	3,776.30	8	−7,536.59	−7,477.56	8,737.45	8,560.34
3. GoM-Specific Probabilities (no Age)	7,873.29	4	−15,738.58	−15,709.06	535.46	328.83
4. Age & GoM-Specific Probabilities	8,169.02	32	−16,274.04	−16,037.89	0.00	0.00

GoM scores but not over age, following the values displayed in the Totals row of Table 7 of the *NAAJ* paper. Model 4 assumes that the sex-specific mortality probabilities increase over GoM scores and over age, following the values displayed in the age-specific rows of Table 7 of the *NAAJ* paper.

The log–likelihood-ratios were generated as the difference in the value of the log–likelihood for each model and the log–likelihood for Model 1. The degrees of freedom (d.f.) were defined as the number of parameters in each model. The AIC (Akaike Information Criterion) was calculated as the log–likelihood-ratio plus 2 times the d.f. The BIC (Bayesian Information Criterion) was calculated as the log–likelihood-ratio plus the product of the d.f and the logarithm of the number of deaths. The best model is the one that has the minimum value of AIC or BIC (indicated with boldface font in Table 6.5); the relative performance of each model is assessed by the difference between its value of AIC or BIC and the minimum value of these statistics (labeled ΔAIC or ΔBIC in Table 6.5). Differences of 10 or more points are regarded as strong evidence in support of the model with the lower AIC or BIC value.

For both sexes and both criteria, Model 4 is overwhelmingly selected as the best model.

To determine whether the GoM scores add significant information beyond the information already available using the age-specific mortality probabilities, we need to compare the value of ΔAIC or ΔBIC for Model 2 with the reference value of 10. For both sexes and both criteria, the values exceed the reference values by a factor of 746–874, indicating that the additional information provided by the GoM scores is huge.

Comparison of Models 2 and 3 provides additional confirmation of the power of the GoM model. The ΔAIC and ΔBIC for Model 2 are each about 30.0 percent smaller than the corresponding value for Model 1 for males and about 46.5 percent smaller for females. The ΔAIC and ΔBIC for Model 3 are each about 97.0 percent smaller than the corresponding value for Model 1 for males and 95.0 percent smaller for females. This means that if one were forced to choose between Models 2 and 3, then Model 3 would be selected as the better model and that the improvement offered by Model 3 would be huge. Model 3 would offer 95–97 percent of the improvement over Model 1 that could ultimately be obtained using Model 4. This would be far in excess of the 30–46 percent improvement offered by Model 2.

The second question is whether the excellent calibration displayed in Figures 6.5 and 6.6 continues when the predictions are stratified by age groups. The results of this stratification are displayed in Figures 6.7 and 6.8 for males and females aged 65–99 years old. The death counts for males at age 100+ fell below the standard CMS cutoff of 11 events and hence were suppressed.

For comparability, females were restricted to the same age range. The aberrant point in Figure 6.6 for the 40–44 percent group turned out to be solely for females aged 100+, which meant that this point was excluded from Figure 6.8.

The labeling of the groups (Pct.Age) in Figures 6.7 and 6.8 combines the lower bounds of the 5-Percent labels in Figures 6.5 and 6.6 with the lower bounds of the age groups in Figures 6.3 and 6.4. Thus, 0.65 identifies persons aged 65–69 years with predicted probabilities in the range 0–4 percent; similarly, 35.95 identifies persons aged 95–99 years with predicted probabilities in the range 35–39 percent. The groups are ordered by increasing predicted probabilities, and within each probability group, by increasing age.

Examination of the results for males and females in Figures 6.7 and 6.8 shows that the largest deviations are for males aged 65–69 (with offsetting

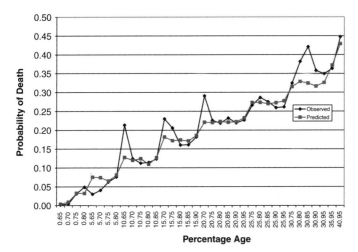

FIGURE 6.7 Observed and Predicted Probabilities of Death, Males Aged 65–99, by Percent Class Intervals and 5-Year Age Group

deviations for 5–9% and 10–14%) and aged 70–74 (with offsetting deviations for 5–9 percent and 15–19 percent), and that these same deviations are not replicated for females.

One possible explanation for the male result involves the design of the NLTCS in which persons who do not have ADL or IADL impairments at

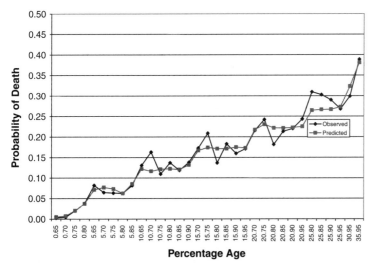

FIGURE 6.8 Observed and Predicted Probabilities of Death, Females Aged 65–99, by Percent Class Intervals and 5-Year Age Group

the time of the survey do not receive the in-person assessment; such persons "screen out" without answering any of the detailed health questions. Thus, the estimates of their GoM scores have substantially larger errors than would be the case for persons who answered most or all of the 95 health questions in the *NAAJ* model, or the 76 questions in the LCC.

To quantify the size of the deviations, we applied linear regression analysis with the observed probabilities regressed on the predicted probabilities, as done above for the data in Figures 6.5 and 6.6, obtaining R-squared values of 0.943 and 0.960, respectively, for males and females, with an overall average of 0.952. As done above, we generated a second set of regressions with the logarithms of the observed probabilities regressed on the logarithms of the predicted probabilities, obtaining R-squared values of 0.958 and 0.984, respectively, with an overall average of 0.971. The implied accuracy is thus in the range 95–97 percent, depending on the form of the regression.

The 32,389 individuals observed in consecutive assessments over the term of this study are a random sample of Medicare enrollees who participated in the National Long-Term Care Survey. Assessments began either in 1982, when the NLTCS started, or at a later date, when the participants were aged 65–69. Because homeownership data was not collected, we do not know how many of these seniors were homeowners. What we do know from Census Bureau data is that more than 70 percent of seniors age 65 are homeowners.

For those preferring medical study validity values, unpublished analyses using out-of-sample data from the Medicare Current Beneficiary Survey yielded an ROC score of 0.8, which for actuarial/medical studies represent a high degree of accuracy.

REVERSE MORTGAGE LOAN PRICING USING THE LONGEVITY COST CALCULATOR

The 76 questions used in the Longevity Cost Calculator are today built into an application form used for life settlements and also into several automated web site applications used by settlement brokers, providers, and financial professionals. At the end of the automated input, all of the relevant morbidity and mortality data needed for a reverse mortgage pricing model are available. The use of this model to determine moveout in lieu of Gompertz-type exponential mortality tables would allow individual-loan-level pricing of reverse mortgages. Homeowners' payments would be tuned to their tenure in the home. Investors would be buying securitized portfolios of loans where the cash inflows for loan maturities and outflows to make payments more closely match the tenure of individual seniors in their homes.

Annual mark-to-market valuations of these portfolios would produce more accurate values. A problem would exist under the auditing and accounting framework until a second methodology for valuation could be agreed on.

For the life settlement sister asset class, there is already an accepted methodology of using third-party life expectancy consultants to estimate an insured's life expectancy using his or her medical records. The underwriter determines debits and credits that are combined into a multiplier that is applied to a standard mortality table. These LE estimates, based on Gompertz exponential large-population mortality tables, are flawed for all the same reasons. But these commercial LEs offer a strong comparative starting point and the alternative valuation methodology needed for mark-to-market revaluation.

EXISTING ACCOUNTING FRAMEWORK

Established business asset valuation measurement is divided into three levels dependent on the credibility and acceptance of the data available to establish the asset's value:

1. *Level-1* measurement is determined by reference to quoted prices for identical assets in the active reference market such as stock exchange–listed prices.
2. *Level-2* measurement is determined by valuation methods using observable data. The valuation methods are the cost approach, present value approach, and the market approach. This method would apply only to valuing settlements after the death of the insureds.
3. *Level-3* measurement is determined by valuation methods using unobservable data. The valuation methods are the cost approach, present value approach, and the market approach. Level 3 is the only appropriate method of measurement for life settlements using the present value approach applied to each loan in a pool.

The framework exists today to create uniformity in reverse mortgage longevity underwriting and related disclosure by applying existing GAAP at the time new loans are originated and existing loans are pooled for securitization and annually at revaluation. These loan portfolios, whether rated or unrated, will require disclosure at the time they are pooled and sold, and subsequently when the pools are individually audited or because they are held for investment by issuers of audited financial statements. For level-3 assets where value is dependent on a future unobservable outcome (the borrowers move out), GAAP requires the use of the best information available,

a first valuation method and then a second independent corroborating valuation methodology. The outcome of these two methodologies is then reconciled and disclosed. Specific relevant accounting doctrine includes AU §328 (previously SAS101), *Auditing Fair Value Measurements and Disclosures* (June 2003); Accounting Standards Codification (ASC) 820.10.05 through 820.10.65 (previously FASB 157), *Fair Value Measurement and Disclosure.*
    AU §328.03 states,

> *ASC glossary term fair value is defined as the price that would be received to sell an asset or paid to transfer a liability in an orderly transaction between market participants at the measurement date. Although GAAP may not prescribe the method for measuring the fair value of an item, it expresses a preference for the use of observable market prices to make that determination.*

Clearly, a life settlement is a "level-3" asset whose value is dependent on an unobservable variable—the future death of the insured.[15] "In the absence of observable market prices, GAAP requires fair value to be based on the best information available in the circumstances."
    AU §328.06 states,

> *Assumptions used in fair value measurements are similar in nature to those required when developing other accounting estimates. However, if observable market prices are not available, GAAP requires that valuation methods incorporate assumptions that marketplace participants would use in their estimates of fair value whenever that information is available without undue cost and effort. If information about market assumptions is not available, an entity may use its own assumptions as long as there are no contrary data indicating that marketplace participants would use different assumptions.*

AU §329.18 goes on to say,

> *Management may have determined that different valuation methods result in a range of significantly different fair value measurements. In such cases, the auditor evaluates how the entity has investigated the reasons for these differences in establishing its fair value measurement.*

    AU §328.23, under the heading *Testing the Entity's Fair Value Measurements and Disclosures*, presents the following:

For example, substantive tests of the fair value measurements may involve (a) testing management's significant assumptions, the valuation model[s], and the underlying data (see paragraphs .26 through .39), (b) developing independent fair value estimates for corroborative purposes (see paragraph .40), or (c) reviewing subsequent events and transactions (see paragraphs .41 and .42).

AU 328.40, under the heading *Developing Independent Fair Value Estimates for Corroborative Purposes* states,

The auditor may make an independent estimate of fair value (for example, by using an auditor-developed model) to corroborate the entity's fair value measurement.[16] When developing an independent estimate using management's assumptions, the auditor evaluates those assumptions as discussed in paragraphs .28 to .37. Instead of using management's assumptions, the auditor may develop his or her own assumptions to make a comparison with management's assumptions. The auditor uses that understanding to ensure that his or her independent estimates take into consideration all significant variables and to evaluate any significant differences from management's estimates. The auditor also should test the data used to develop the fair value measurements and disclosures as discussed in paragraph .39.

SUGGESTED GAAP-COMPLIANT METHODOLOGY TO STANDARDIZE LIFE SETTLEMENT UNDERWRITING

Because AU §328 will require auditors to employ two valuation methodologies, the most cost-efficient way to comply will be to use a standardized Longevity Cost Calculator[TM]–compliant questionnaire to yield an LCC LE at the time of loan application or at the time of mandatory loan counseling. Once a second methodology has been agreed on, that methodology will be used at origination to develop a "shadow pricing" for each loan. At the time of annual audit, this will allow the actual-versus-expected values for each loan's moveout to be evaluated and ranked accordingly. The moveout evaluations will be conducted using Bayesian Information Criterion (BIC) measures of goodness of fit of the actual-to-expected probabilities of moveout computed separately for each moveout model using the same pool of loans. Kass and Raftery[17,18] showed how BIC values can be used (1) to rank the various moveout models and (2) to generate optimal weighted averages of the outputs of the various moveout models. The resultant weighted averaging can then be applied to each individual loan, and to the aggregate of all loans, in annually revaluing each portfolio. The BIC weights can be updated each year as additional information on the actual number of moveouts in that year becomes available. Over time, this will give greater weight to the better performing models. Disclosure of this methodology at portfolio formulation and annually will create transparency into these longevity valued asset transactions for investors.

SUMMARY

For the past 30 years, reverse mortgage products of all types have been improperly priced using large population mortality tables. Shifting to individual loan pricing based on more accurate individual moveout will benefit seniors receiving reverse mortgages, the taxpayers that guarantee portfolio performance, and investors who buy interests in securitized loan pools. This product design change will be driven by the need to annually revalue loan portfolios to comply with mark-to-market fair value auditing and accounting standards.

BHUYAN'S FINAL POINTS

- Enhancing the methods of underwriting reverse mortgage loans will result in a more attractive product for borrowers and subsequently for institutional investors.

- Population data is simply too general to use as a basis to price sophisticated financial instruments.

- A single, or small number of, generally accepted valuation and actuarial metrics for all *life-linked* assets, such as life settlements and reverse mortgages, is critical to build transparency in the asset class.

- Currently, multiple actuarial tables and combinations of tables are used to price loans, which will prevent these assets from achieving the benefits of mass demand through securitization.

NOTES

1. This was first described in J. W. Vaupel, K. G. Manton, and E. Stallard, "The Impact of Heterogeneity in Individual Frailty on the Dynamics of Mortality," *Demography* 16(3): 439–454, 1979. Further evidence was provided in I. A. Iachine, N. V. Holm, J. R. Harris, A. Z. Begun, M. K. Iachina, M. Laitinen, J. Kaprio, and A. I. Yashin, "How Heritable Is Individual Susceptibility to Death? The Results of an Analysis of Survival Data on Danish, Swedish and Finnish Twins," *Twin Research* 1: 196–205, 1998.

2. Under a HIPAA Business Associate Agreement, Life Settlement Financial, LLC (LSF) has examined approximately 1,000 resident sets of assessment data spanning up to seven calendar years. This evaluation and data compilation was done primarily to revalidate LSF's Longevity Cost Calculator™ (LCC). Thirty-one of the questions in the Vigilan assessment tool directly map to the 76 questions in the LCC. A byproduct of this revaluation was the observation that seniors entering assisted living have typically lost between two and three ADLs. Statistically, the average stay by a senior in an assisted-living community is 25 months. They leave either because of death or because they are moved to a skilled nursing facility.

3. B. Gompertz, "On the Nature of the Function Expressive of the Law of Human Mortality, and on a New Mode of Determining the Value of Life Contingencies," *Philosophical Transactions of the Royal Society of London* 115: 513–583, 1825.

4. The Gompertz law can be written with three elements: a continuous exponential function of age, a, with a growth constant β, and a proportionality constant α. The Gompertz law has been evaluated in numerous studies. Several problems have been identified: (1) The fitted Gompertz function tends to overestimate mortality above about 80–90 years of age. (2) The Gompertz "constants" (α and β) are not really constant; they differ from one population to another and over calendar time and cohort within a given population. (3) The numerical values of α and β are negatively correlated when calculated for populations with a broad range of mortality conditions. Despite these problems, the Gompertz function provides a useful approximation to the age-specific mortality probabilities, qa, and an even better approximation to the age-specific mortality "hazard rates," μa, defined as $\mu a = -\ln(1 - qa)$, which can be solved for qa, using $(a = \alpha \exp(\beta a)$. Note that qa is the probability that a person alive at exact age a will die prior to exact age $a + 1$. Typical increases in qa are in the range of 8–10 percent per year.

5. See W. H. Wetterstrand, "Parametric Models for Life Insurance Mortality Data: Gompertz's Law over Time," *Transactions of the Society of Actuaries* 33: 443–468, 1981; and S. J. Olshansky, and B. A. Carnes, "Ever Since Gompertz," *Demography* 34(1): 1–15, 1997.

6. See B. L. Strehler, and A. S. Mildvan, "General Theory of Mortality and Aging." *Science* 132(3418): 14–21, 1960; and L. A. Gavrilov, and N. S.

Gavrilova, "The Reliability Theory of Aging and Longevity," *Journal of Theoretical Biology* 213: 527–545, 2001.

7. *Ibid.*

8. This was first described in J. W. Vaupel, K. G. Manton, and E. Stallard, "The Impact of Heterogeneity in Individual Frailty on the Dynamics of Mortality," *Demography* 16(3): 439–454, 1979. Further evidence was provided in I. A. Iachine, N. V. Holm, J. R. Harris, A. Z. Begun, M. K. Iachina, M. Laitinen, J. Kaprio, and A. I. Yashin, "How Heritable Is Individual Susceptibility to Death? The Results of an Analysis of Survival Data on Danish, Swedish and Finnish Twins," *Twin Research* 1: 196–205, 1998.

9. Eric Stallard, Trajectories of Morbidity, Disability, and Mortality Among the U.S. Elderly Population: Evidence from the 1984–1999 NLTCS.

10. The previously mentioned paper was first peer reviewed before presentation at *The Living to 100 and Beyond Symposium* sponsored by the Society of Actuaries, January 12–14, 2005. The conference committee referred the paper for further peer review and consideration for publication in the *North American Actuarial Journal.*

11. www.lifesettlementfinancial.com/the-longevity-cost-calculator.html.

12. Eric Stallard, *NAAJ* paper, Appendix, pp. 49–50, "NLTCS Variables, Log-Likelihood Values, and Chi-Squared Statistics by Variable, by Sex."

13. L. H. Longley-Cook, *An Introduction to Credibility Theory*, Casualty Actuarial Society, 1962, p. 9.

14. L. H. Longley-Cook, *An Introduction to Credibility Theory*, Casualty Actuarial Society, 1962, p. 9.

15. PCAOB Standing Advisory Group Meeting, October 14–15, 2009, "Auditing Fair Value Measurements and Using the Work of a Specialist," paper developed by the staff of the Office of the Chief Auditor.

16. ACS 820-10-35-52 sets forth the parameters for level-3 assets where fair value is determined from unobservable future events.

17. See AU §329, *Analytical Procedures.*

18. See equations (9), (16), and (18) in R. E. Kass and A. E. Raftery, "Bayes Factors," *Journal of the American Statistical Association* 90(430): 773–795, 1995. Note that BIC values can be generated using various approaches to measuring goodness of fit, including chi-squared statistics and regression-based R^2-statistics.

CHAPTER 7

Risk Mitigation

Available Hedges and Products in Development for Risk Transfer

Chris DeSilva
Managing Partner, Risk Capital Partners, LLC

*S*ecuritization is a standard exit strategy in the industry for the liquidity it provides originators as well as the ample demand from end investors. As with many existing mortgage products, the timing of cash flows for reverse mortgages can be better managed by pooling and structuring all the underlying collateral. A tighter payment window provides transparency for assessing risk-adjusted returns. Despite the benefits of securitization, reverse mortgage deals have been limited since the first deal in 1999, SASCO 99-RM1.

- There is no existing software (e.g., INTEX) that can easily model reverse mortgage cash flows.
- There are no early-period cash flows or early current interest from the collateral.
- Given the early product stage of reverses, deal processing is slow relative to traditional loan and deal processing.

The issue with securitized product is that it is an end product, meaning that investors in reverse mortgages must have the collateral securitized and then repurchase the exact tranche that fits their risk profile (as shown in Figure 7.1). This is somewhat backward thinking: Those looking to securitize may actually be seeking ways to mitigate crossover risk prior to putting the collateral in a deal structure. Furthermore, many investors may want to

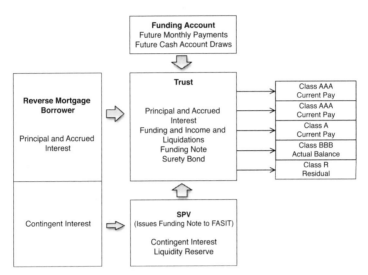

FIGURE 7.1 SASCO 99-RM1

hold reverse mortgages on their balance sheets without indirectly paying for the transaction costs and other banking and structuring fees associated with securitization when they purchase a part of the deal.

The exact structures that exist and the mechanics of the trusts are beyond the scope of this discussion.

HEDGING CROSSOVER COMPONENTS IN THE CAPITAL MARKETS

From the diagram in Figure 7.2 it is clear that as interest rates rise, Home Price Appreciation (HPA) slows and can even turn negative, which in turn accelerates the probability of crossover. There are highly liquid interest rate derivative products that can minimize the risk from rising rates. Given the correlation between interest rates and home prices, interest rate derivatives can hedge two of the three main components in crossover risk: home price depreciation, and the acceleration in loan accrual.

An investor could either go short swaps or purchase caps (call options on interest rates), which economically benefit as interest rates rise, offsetting the problems of declining home prices and accelerating loan accrual. There are costs and benefits to swaps and caps, as shown in Table 7.1, but both provide a reasonable hedging solution.

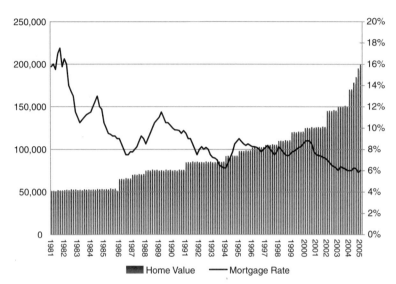

FIGURE 7.2 Home Prices versus Mortgage Rates
Source: CME Group, Case-Shiller contracts.

The problem with using only interest rate derivatives to hedge HPA is the basis risk between rates and HPA; home prices often lag interest rates or deviate completely. The current environment provides a perfect example. During 2008–2009, the Federal Reserve moved interest rates to historical lows; and longer-duration interest rates also followed suit. However, home prices experienced one of the largest collapses in history during this same period. In this instance, any interest rate hedge would have lost money while crossover risk would have increased. Any gain from a deceleration in loan accrual would have been more than offset by these two larger factors. There are purer ways to hedge the HPA component of crossover risk, and eliminate basis.

TABLE 7.1 Pros and Cons of Swaps and Caps

Hedge	Pros	Cons
Short Swaps	Low cost	Difficult to establish hedge ratio
	Easy to value and mark	Possible downside
Long Caps	Downside limited to premium	High cost
		Managing convexity or gamma

Metropolitan Area	October 2009 Level	October/ September Change (%)	September/August Change (%)	1-Year Change (%)
Atlanta	110.12	−1.0%	0.0%	−8.1%
Boston	154.70	−0.6%	−0.2%	−2.8%
Charlotte	119.05	−0.7%	−0.7%	−7.0%
Chicago	130.78	−1.0%	1.2%	−10.1%
Cleveland	104.97	−0.7%	−1.6%	−3.5%
Dallas	119.90	−0.6%	−0.7%	−0.6%
Denver	128.91	−0.4%	−0.5%	−0.1%
Detroit	73.07	0.2%	1.8%	−15.1%
Las Vegas	104.70	−0.1%	−0.9%	−26.6%
Los Angeles	168.43	0.3%	0.8%	−6.3%
Miami	149.09	−0.4%	0.5%	−14.0%
Minneapolis	124.51	−0.5%	1.9%	−8.4%
New York	175.01	0.0%	−0.1%	−7.7%
Phoenix	110.71	1.3%	0.8%	−18.1%
Portland	149.88	0.1%	−0.5%	−9.9%
San Diego	155.37	0.4%	0.9%	−2.4%
San Francisco	135.81	1.2%	1.3%	−2.6%
Seattle	149.26	0.2%	−0.4%	−12.4%
Tampa	140.27	−1.6%	−0.6%	−15.2%
Washington	179.71	−0.4%	0.5%	−2.8%
Composite—10	158.82	0.0%	0.5%	−6.4%
Composite—20	146.58	0.0%	0.4%	−7.3%

FIGURE 7.3 Home Price Index Levels (as of October 2009)
Source: Standard & Poor's and Fiserv.

Housing Derivatives

In the early days of reverse mortgages, there were no capital markets products to strictly hedge home price appreciation risk (Figure 7.3). Since 2006, at the height of the most recent housing bubble, several products have emerged that provide better hedging solutions.[1] Most housing derivatives will be better hedges for home price appreciation than interest derivatives because of the underlying basis between interest rates and HPA that can occur during high-sigma events such as the credit crisis of 2008.

Several financial products are available in today's markets:

- *HPA futures and options:* The Chicago Mercantile Exchange (CME) has the purest play for HPA. The S&P/Case-Shiller index, shown in Figure 7.4, measures the residential housing market in 20 metropolitan

FIGURE 7.4 S&P/Case-Shiller Home Price Indices
Source: Standard & Poor's and Fiserv.

areas, and tracks the changes on a monthly basis. The Exchange facilitates the trading of both futures and options on specific metropolitan areas, and the weighted composite index.

- *Swaps:* There are several swaps that investors can purchase (meaning to get short credit in our case) to hedge declines in housing prices. The underlying theory is that swap spreads widen in sympathy to a weakness in housing. Again, there is basis in this product because swaps can trade on a technical basis rather than directly correlate to housing prices. For example, credit swaps can tighten, leading to losses for the hedge, when there is an overwhelming demand for spread products, a condition that existed from 2005–2007. HPA can be stagnant in such cases while the hedges would lose money in the short-term.

  A scenario that is more frequent is for swap spreads to widen to exogenous shocks. There are several instances where non-housing occurrences led to spreads widening, for example, the insolvency of Long-Term Capital Management, the bankruptcy of WorldCom, and the Enron debacle (Figure 7.5). Although any hedge would have gained during these occurrences, the added layer of risk must be recognized and managed.

  These occurrences in the credit markets are atypical, but these atypical events are exactly what active investors need to hedge.

In addition, framing the product decision process is complex:

- The cost of carry needs to be weighed against the value at risk.
- Hedge ratios must be established and back-tested.
- Economics should be fully calculated for every hedge mix and optimized.

A full cost/benefit analysis is crucial in launching any hedge program of this scope, as shown in Table 7.2.

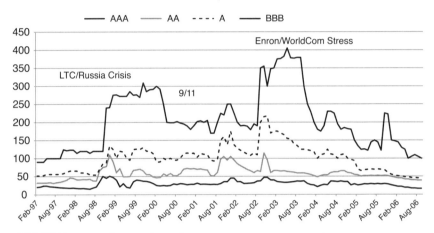

FIGURE 7.5   HEL Floating Spreads

INSURANCE SOLUTIONS

As discussed, the underwriting criteria for reverse mortgages are loan-to-value and the age of the borrower. Given that the current value of the home is determined by market, the driver for the amount of the loan should be an exercise in mobility and mortality. This very fact gives support to the increasing need for insurance companies to become more involved with the pricing and risk management of the reverse mortgages. With longstanding research and the latest actuarial models, life companies should add significant value to the reverse mortgage process.

Mortality Coverage

Actuarial risk is the component of crossover risk that investors will find most challenging to hedge. This expertise is usually outside the scope of the financial companies that are engaged in mortgage lending. However, life

TABLE 7.2   Cost/Benefit Analysis

Types of Swaps	Pro's	Con's
Total Return Swap: Agreed upon Housing index is utilized	No costs for unwind Ease of use for systems & reporting	High transaction costs: bid/ask spread . . . 4 to 6 bps
ABX.HE: 20 representative deals w/5 sub-indices introduced every 6 months	Market liquidity and price transparency	Avg. Correlation = 49%

companies have been managing and modeling this risk for decades, and are poised to translate this experience to offer risk transfer coverages for the reverse mortgage industry.

Example Coverage Abstract A *reverse mortgage insurance* policy can cover newly originated reverse mortgage loans or protect against risks relating to a portfolio of existing reverse mortgage loans. The insurance would indemnify against losses incurred when proceeds from the sale of the mortgaged property fail to satisfy the then-outstanding principal and interest.

For a given loan, losses would be measured as of the reverse mortgage loan due date, which we anticipate being the earlier of:

- The date of death of the last surviving reverse mortgage borrower;
- The date of the sale of the mortgaged property or other conveyance of its title;
- The date on which the reverse mortgage borrower violates any applicable loan covenants (e.g. failure to pay taxes and insurance); or
- The date on which the mortgaged property ceases to be the principal residence of all borrowers for a period longer than 12 consecutive months.

Losses resulting from any one or a combination of the following situations could be covered:

- The value of the property fails to appreciate at the expected rate; and/or
- The reverse mortgage borrower remains in the mortgaged property longer than expected, resulting in higher-than-expected accrued interest; and/or
- Assuming that the reverse mortgage is a floating rate loan, interest rates increase more than expected during the life of the loan, resulting in higher-than-expected accrued interest.

Premium Rates We would expect premium to be calculated as follows:

- *Reverse mortgage insurance attaching as new loans incept:* A combination of an upfront amount and ongoing basis points (bps) running. We will consider a fixed premium rate for all loans or a loan-by-loan computation, based on the borrower's age and gender, the interest rate, and the property appreciation rate applied.
- *Reverse mortgage insurance for an existing portfolio of loans:* An upfront minimum and deposit premium with an adjustment based on actual exposure.

Please see Table 7.3 for additional specifics.

TABLE 7.3 Example Coverage Terms

Criterion	Example Guidelines
Home Value Limit	Maximum—$3 to 5 million Minimum—None
Maximum Initial Loan Amount	Maximum initial loan amount is computed by multiplying the agreed LTV for a borrower of a defined age/gender by the initial home value.
Age Requirement	Refer to state limitations. Otherwise, the youngest borrower should be at least 60 years old. Maximum of 2 borrowers
FICO Requirements	TBD
Income or Credit Qualifications	TBD
Property Valuations	Standard appraisal required. Property inspection required.
Property Types	Owner occupied—primary residence only. 1-4 unit single family residences, condos, PUDs 2nd homes possible Manufactured housing and unique property types ineligible.
Property Locations	Available in 50 states and as permitted by state regulations.
Lien Position	First lien
Ownership	Any existing mortgage debt must be paid off either with proceeds from the reverse mortgage or by the homeowner from other funds.
Interest Rate	TBA No periodic cap [10%] lifetime cap over initial rate
Disbursement Options	One-time lump sum payment Tenure (fixed payment amounts on regular (monthly or quarterly basis) schedule until due date or for a fixed time period Line Of Credit
Set Asides	Escrow must be established for the completion of required repairs not completed prior to funding. (Min/Max standards TBD)
Prepayment	No prepayment penalty
Payment of Claims	Option to purchase loan when the outstanding balance is __% (TBD) of the original home value. See Exhibit A for MI claim calculation.
Monthly Loan Activity Reporting	Must report status of following on a monthly basis: Loan Balance

	Applicable interest rate
	Amount of credit available
	Payoff
	Issuance of repayment notice to borrower
	Status of loans in default
	Confirmation on verification of occupancy.
Occupancy & Property Maintenance	Annual written certification of borrower occupancy.
	Monthly Social Security sweep and quarterly contact with borrower.
	Servicer to request borrower to provide, in writing, absences from property in excess of two months.
	Annual drive-by inspections of property to begin in 4th year after origination. Complete Property Inspection report and photo of property for loan file.
Real Estate Taxes and Insurance	Must confirm taxes and insurance are current on an annual basis.
	If borrower doesn't pay, servicer makes payments and adds to loan balance. Term/tenure plans will have payments reduced.
	Non-payment of taxes and insurance are excluded from insurance cover.
Repairs	Servicer must confirm repairs are completed per appraiser post closing in timely manner (maximum 12 months after loan closing).

Medical Underwriting

Better product design could be available via medical underwriting, which is common in the well-entrenched life products like life insurance and annuities. Although this approach has faced resistance due to ethical and regulatory issues, there is growing favor for this solution because of its many benefits, the primary being the possibility of more money for seniors that need home equity. As cash flow uncertainty decreases from better principal windows, investor demand would increase, thereby passing on some of the benefits directly to borrowers.

Benefits of Cross-Correlation

Life companies can also benefit from absorbing the actuarial risk embedded in reverse mortgages. Their balance sheet has assets such as life insurance policies that can directly offset the risk of mortality extension.

SUMMARY

In summary, reverse mortgages should experience rapid growth as the large aging population increasingly taps home equity to provide for retirement needs. Moreover, crossover risk must be appropriately managed for the faster growing segment of nonconforming reverse mortgages. Finally, existing products in capital markets together with the actuarial expertise in the life industry can craft viable reverse mortgage products for the benefit of both borrowers and investors.

BHUYAN'S FINAL POINTS

- Securitization of *life-linked* assets such as reverse mortgages and life settlements will allow a larger number of investors around the world to achieve high risk-adjusted returns while limiting their exposure to traditional asset classes such as equities.

- There are a number of challenges in the securitization of such assets, such as the unpredictability of cash flows, high frictional and administrative costs, as well as a lack of education on these products.

- Although an investor may hedge out some of the risk associated with reverse mortgages through housing derivatives or longevity insurance, enhancing the accuracy of actuarial underwriting and pricing loans off of more conservative tables are the least expensive and most efficient ways to manage risk.

- With housing prices in the United States falling dramatically since the end of 2007, the timing of reverse mortgage investments may be ideal.

NOTE

1. One of the most notable trades by modern-day hedge funds, which eventually went to press as "The Greatest Trade Ever" by Gregory Zuckerman, was executed in HPA derivatives. John Paulson's fund reaped $15 billion in 2007 buying credit default swaps on collateralized debt obligations constructed from mortgage loans.

CHAPTER 8

Criteria for Rating U.K. Reverse Mortgage–Backed Securities

Victoria Johnstone, Karen Naylor, Apea Koranteng, Kai Gilkes & Andrea Quirk
Analysts, Standard & Poor's

Bond issuance based on the future cash flows generated by reverse mort-gage loans is a recent innovation in the U.K. mortgage-backed securities market. Nevertheless, as homeownership and the elderly population stead-ily expand in the U.K., there is significant scope for growth in the demand for reverse mortgage–type products.

There are more than 10.8 million people in the U.K. over pensionable age, a number forecast to increase dramatically as life expectancy increases and birth rates fall. This projected growth, coupled with overall house price increases, has resulted in a substantial number of elderly borrowers with a sig-nificant amount of available equity in their homes. In fact, the Council of Mortgage Lenders recently reported that older homeowners utilize only ap-proximately 1 percent of the £400 billion of equity in their homes. Not surpris-ingly, market participants expect a significant increase in activity in this asset class, given the extent of untapped home equity among these homeowners.

This chapter sets out Standard & Poor's approach to rating securitiza-tions of the reverse mortgage asset class.

OVERVIEW OF REVERSE (EQUITY RELEASE) MORTGAGES

A reverse (or *equity release*) mortgage is a product designed for older home-owners who wish to release a portion of the equity in their property without having to sell their home and move. In its typical form, a percentage of the value of the borrower's home is advanced as a cash lump sum and the borrower continues to own and occupy the property. The borrower makes no monthly repayments, and there is no defined loan term. All accrued interest is capitalized into the principal balance of the loan, and repayment of the accrued loan amount is required only when the property is sold.

The sale of the property occurs when the borrower dies (mortality), moves out of the house (typically into long-term care due to ill health), sells voluntarily, or defaults under the terms and conditions of the loan agreement (e.g., fails to maintain building's insurance coverage or abandons the property). Proceeds from the sale of the property are then used to repay the outstanding loan balance.

Reverse mortgage loans have only recently appeared on the U.K. mortgage market, and are offered by few lenders at present. Borrowers taking advantage of these types of products have generally repaid their regular mortgages in full, and use the proceeds from the reverse mortgage loan for a variety of purposes (e.g., as a supplemental income, a means to finance a significant purchase or home, and quality of life improvements).

The greatest risk to a lender extending this type of mortgage loan is that the accrued loan amount outstanding exceeds the sale proceeds from the property (commonly referred to as the *crossover point*). Figure 8.1 illustrates the change in the Loan-to-Value LTV ratio over time for two borrowers with a home initially valued at 100. One borrower is advanced 20 percent of the home value, the other 80 percent. Both loans are assumed to accrue interest at 8 percent, and the overall annual price increase of the underlying property asset is assumed to be 2 percent. If the house sale occurs before the crossover point, the lender will receive the full loan balance on sale. If the house sale occurs after the crossover point, the lender will receive only the house sale proceeds less costs.

Note that the crossover point occurs earlier for the larger initial LTV. Given this relationship, the amount initially advanced to a borrower is determined on the basis of (1) the borrower's estimated life expectancy and (2) the expected future value of the property upon the borrower's death. In general, the older the borrower, the higher the LTV the lender will consider.

REVERSE MORTGAGE–BACKED SECURITIZATION

Standard & Poor's overall approach to risk evaluation of reverse mortgage–backed securities (RVMBS) differs substantially from RMBS. Unlike RMBS transactions, in which the borrower is required to make regular payments, the receipt of cash from a reverse mortgage occurs only following the sale of

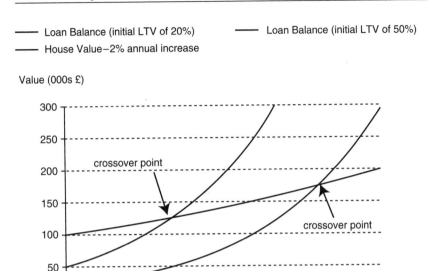

—— Loan Balance (initial LTV of 20%)   —— Loan Balance (initial LTV of 50%)
—— House Value–2% annual increase

FIGURE 8.1   Reverse Mortgage Loan Accrual

the property, primarily when the borrower dies or moves out. Therefore, assumptions based on the timing of the borrower's death, moveout (due to ill health and voluntary prepayments), and house price appreciation are central to Standard & Poor's analysis of the cash flow from a portfolio of reverse mortgage loans.

MORTALITY ASSUMPTIONS

The Continuous Mortality Investigation (CMI) Bureau publishes standardized probability tables that detail the timing of future mortality based on the age and gender of an individual. In general, Standard & Poor's considers the latest available tables based on the mortality experience of insured lives from group pension schemes, weighted by the pension amounts, as the most appropriate base tables to use for this product type. In the report entitled "Continuous Mortality Investigation Report No. 16, The Mortality of Pensioners in Insured Group Pension Schemes, 1991–94," published by the CMI, the PMA92 and PFA92 mortality tables describe male and female mortality, respectively.

Mortality rates for all age groups have significantly improved since 1992, and therefore the base tables are adjusted in the analysis to reflect these improvements. In addition, borrower mortality rates are expected to continue to improve in the future. Standard & Poor's stresses these further improvement predictions, and increases the delay in overall borrower mortality at higher rating levels in some stress scenarios. Although the CMI mortality tables have been standardized for internal cash flow analysis purposes, other adjustments to the base tables may be considered in the context of a particular transaction. In addition, if the demographics of a particular portfolio of borrowers differ substantially from the population described in the PMA92/PFA92 tables, alternative tables can be used.

PREPAYMENT ASSUMPTIONS

The usual types of prepayment observed in RMBS pools, such as voluntary moveouts due to changing property needs, and refinancing to a more attractive loan pricing, should occur with less frequency in a reverse mortgage pool.

Recipients of reverse mortgage loans are less likely to move purely for lifestyle reasons, given that one of the main attractions of the reverse mortgage product is that the borrower can remain in his or her home. Although some level of prepayments due to voluntary moveouts will still occur in reverse mortgage pools, it is likely to be more prevalent among younger borrowers.

Refinancing in prime RMBS transactions is primarily driven by changes in interest rates. Given that there are no regular and ongoing payments to make on a reverse mortgage loan, and competition to originate this product has not been particularly intense among mortgage lenders to date, prepayments as a result of refinancing are likely to be less frequent in a reverse mortgage pool. Reverse mortgage prepayments are most likely to occur when a borrower relocates into long-term care as a result of failing health, a scenario that is less common in RMBS.

Standard & Poor's applies a variety of age-sensitive prepayment functions at each rating level. Three examples are given in Figure 8.2.

These functions combine the prepayments due to voluntary moveouts and relocations to long-term-care accommodation into a blended rate for each age. Given that the relative influence of these two prepayment types will be age sensitive, the blended rate changes as a function of borrower age. For example, the intermediate prepayment rate associated with younger borrowers captures the assumption that these borrowers are more likely to prepay as the result of a voluntary move. The increase in the prepayment rate after age 75 captures the assumption that older borrowers are more

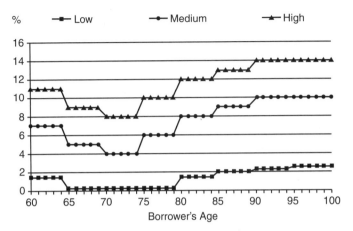

FIGURE 8.2 Annual Prepayment Rates Applied over Changes in
Borrower Age

likely to move into long-term care as a result of failing health. These prepayment rates are modeled dynamically over the transaction as the surviving borrowers increase in age. Note that the curves shown in Figure 8.2 are
examples only, and can be altered to test a transaction's sensitivity to different prepayment rates.

HOUSE PRICE INCREASE ASSUMPTIONS

Standard & Poor's will divide the life of the transaction into four distinct time
periods, each characterized by a different *house price increase (HPI)* assumption. A general summary as to the HPI assumptions used in each of these time
periods is provided below. The liability structure of the transaction in question is crucial in the selection of both the timing and severity of these house
price stresses, and consequently, they should be used merely as a guide. In all
cases, the HPI assumes zero inflation, and therefore any analysis of historical
house prices is adjusted for the influence of the retail price index.
    Standard & Poor's house price analyses rely on data from both the
Halifax and Nationwide Building Society house price indices, both of which
calculate a mix-adjusted house price index. The mix adjustment accounts
for the relative number of different sale types (e.g., flats, detached houses,
maisonettes) that contribute to the index in a particular time period. If the
property mix of a reverse mortgage pool is substantially weighted toward
one particular type (e.g., sheltered housing, etc.), the effect of this weighting
may influence the HPI modeled for the transaction.

HPI in Year 1

The HPI modeled in the first year of the transaction is generally determined from an analysis of the current house price index predictions for the following year.

HPI in Years 2–4

As in the case of RMBS, a recession that influences the resale value of properties is assumed to occur in the early years of the transaction. In addition, the resale value of the property is assumed to decrease in a linear fashion over the three-year period. The final market value declines at the end of the three-year period are the same as those used in RMBS transactions, where the severity of the decrease in house prices is both region and rating dependant (see Table 8.1). The market value decline assumptions for loans in the south (i.e., southeast, including London, southwest and East Anglia) are greater than those assigned to loans in the north (East Midlands, West Midlands, northwest, Yorkshire and Humberside, north, Wales, Scotland, and Northern Ireland). This difference is modeled by assuming a blended house price decrease based on the geographic distribution of the borrowers in a particular gender and age band.

HPI in Years 5–15

A post-recession recovery period is assumed to occur from the end of the recession to the end of year 15. The annual HPI required for this part of the transaction is tested against the historical likelihood of obtaining such an increase, to a confidence level consistent with a particular rating category.

TABLE 8.1 Market Value Decline Assumptions

Rating	South Market Value Decline (% of Total Decrease)	South Market Value Decline (% of Annualized Decrease over a Three-Year Period)	North Market Value Decline (% of Total Decrease)	North Market Value Decline (% of Annualized Decrease over a Three-Year Period)
AAA	47	19.1	25	9.1
AA	40	15.7	22	8.0
A	35	13.4	19	6.8
BBB	30	11.2	16	5.7

The assessment of historical HPI hinges on a detailed analysis of both the Nationwide and Halifax house price indices. Here, annual HPI estimates are simulated using historical annual HPIs observed in non-recessionary periods for both north and south regions. Multiple simulations allow for the construction of probability distributions of annualized HPI.

For each rating scenario, the probability of HPI falling below a certain level over the 11-year period from years 5 to 15 is benchmarked against the 11-year probability of a corporate default for that rating level. To attain a particular rating, the probability of obtaining the required HPI over the 11-year period must not exceed this benchmark probability. The corporate default probabilities provide a one-tailed confidence interval on the distribution at each rating level, and as such describe a rating-dependent likelihood of an event occurring.

HPI in Years 16 to Legal Final Maturity Date

A stressed house price increase is assumed to occur for the remaining life of the transaction. The stressed house price increase from year 16 is assumed to be 33 percent of the post-recession estimates obtained for the 5-to-15-year period.

COSTS AND SALE PERIOD

The fixed costs associated with the sale of the property are assumed to be 4 percent of the house value. This figure includes all costs and fees resulting from the administration, maintenance, and sale of the property. The time from the borrower's death, moveout, or default to the receipt of the proceeds from the sale of the property is assumed to be approximately 12 months.

SUMMARY

There are a number of specific structural and legal issues pertinent to reverse mortgage transactions that need careful consideration in the rating process. First, cash is generated from a reverse mortgage pool only when properties are sold due to borrower mortality or moveout, with no receipt of regular monthly payments. This feature creates certain structural challenges if the notes backed by the reverse mortgage loan pool require scheduled principal repayments and interest payments, as there is the potential for large timing mismatches between the asset cash flow and the liability commitments.

In a low-prepayment scenario, most of the cash receipts are likely to coincide with the peak of the mortality distribution. Considerable early liquidity stress is created if the peak occurs in the later years of the transaction. In a high-prepayment scenario, borrowers prepay their outstanding loans prior to the date predicted by the mortality curve, potentially creating negative carry. A structure must be able to withstand such liquidity and negative carry stresses, to the level required by the desired rating.

Finally, reverse mortgage loans are likely to be smaller than residential mortgage loans, and are therefore more likely to be regulated by the Consumer Credit Act. Any breach of these regulations can compromise the enforceability of the loan, and as a result, Standard & Poor's will expect transaction.

BHUYAN'S FINAL POINTS

- Demographic and economic changes within the United Kingdom are attracting both financial institutions and consumers to the reverse mortgage product.

- Given the typical life cycle of a financial instrument, the issuance of bonds linked to reverse mortgages would be a logical next step in the market provided there is sufficient demand among institutional investors.

- Rating agencies such as Standard & Poor's must continue to refine their methodology of assessing the risks of such structured products and the underlying loans.

- More accurate and robust actuarial data, especially that of older homeowners, will result in more accurate assessments of risk as longevity risk, not credit risk, is the primary determinant of pricing these securities.

Three

Tax Treatment

CHAPTER 9

U.S. Federal Income Tax Aspects of Reverse Mortgages

Micah Bloomfield
Partner, Stroock & Stroock & Lavan LLP

Reverse mortgages are subject to a number of special provisions under the U.S. Internal Revenue Code of 1986, as amended (the "Code"), that generally are not applicable to traditional residential mortgage loans. The differences in tax treatment affect both the borrowers under reverse mortgages and the financial institutions that provide capital to fund these loans. Borrowers are likely to have a far harder time securing a deduction for reverse mortgage interest than interest on a traditional mortgage. This is because reverse mortgage interest is subject to significantly more stringent deductibility restrictions than interest on traditional residential mortgages. These restrictions affect both the amount and the timing of reverse mortgage interest deductions and, in the case of many borrowers, are likely to significantly impair the after tax economic utility of the deductions.

In addition to restrictions on deductibility of interest, reverse mortgage loans are subject to unique rules governing their use in securitizations involving real estate mortgage investment conduits ("REMICs"). Until recently, the REMIC rules did not permit reverse mortgage loans to be used in REMIC securitizations. Although these restrictions were removed by the American Jobs Creation Act of 2004 (P.L. 108-357) (the "Jobs Act"), the modified REMIC rules are likely to present potential investors and issuers with a slew of challenging considerations.

This chapter discusses these and certain other unique U.S. federal income tax aspects of reverse mortgages and potential related issues.

WHAT IS A REVERSE MORTGAGE?

Reverse mortgage loans are typically made to elderly individuals who own and occupy their own homes. These loans are intended to allow these individuals to convert some or all of the equity in their houses into an income stream that can be used to meet current expenses, without having to sell the house. When a reverse mortgage is made, the lender typically commits itself to lend an amount not in excess of a certain percentage of the appraised value of the property. The loan is generally paid to the borrower in installments over a period of time.

Interest on a reverse mortgage loan typically is added to the outstanding loan balance as it accrues. Unlike traditional mortgage loans, which have a stated maturity date, reverse mortgages generally do not have a fixed maturity date and do not need to be repaid until the occurrence of one or more "maturity" events. These events typically include the death of the borrower, sale of the residence securing the loan, or the borrower ceasing to use the home as a principal residence. Reverse mortgages are typically repaid with the proceeds from the sale of the property securing the loan.

DEDUCTIBILITY OF INTEREST PAYMENTS ON REVERSE MORTGAGES

Individuals generally are allowed to deduct for U.S. federal income tax purposes interest on two categories of debt secured by their personal residence: acquisition indebtedness and home equity indebtedness.[1] *Acquisition indebtedness* includes any debt incurred in acquiring, constructing, or substantially improving a qualified residence that is secured by such residence.[2] *Home equity indebtedness* is any indebtedness, other than acquisition indebtedness, that is secured by a qualified residence.[3] A *primary residence* includes the primary residence of a taxpayer and one secondary residence.[4]

Reverse mortgages generally do not qualify as acquisition indebtedness, because these types of loans are usually incurred by elderly persons to meet living expenses, and not to acquire or improve real estate.[5] Accordingly, in most cases reverse mortgages are likely to be treated only as home equity indebtedness for U.S. federal income tax purposes. Any interest accruing with respect to reverse mortgage loans is thus likely subject to the same restrictions on deductibility as are applicable to home equity indebtedness.

The Code places far greater limits on deductions for interest on home equity indebtedness than interest on acquisition indebtedness. In the case of debt qualifying as acquisition indebtedness, interest is deductible on the aggregate amount of such debt up to $1,000,000 ($500,000 in the case of a married individual filing a joint return).[6] When it comes to home equity indebtedness, however, interest is deductible with respect to a portion of such debt equal to the lesser of $100,000 ($50,000 in the case of married individuals filing a separate return) or an amount (not less than zero) equal to the difference between the fair market value of the qualified residence securing the home equity indebtedness and the aggregate amount of acquisition indebtedness with respect to such residence.[7]

The Internal Revenue Service has imposed additional restrictions on the deductibility of interest on reverse mortgage loans. It has ruled that borrowers that use the cash receipts and disbursements method of accounting[8] cannot deduct interest that accrues on a reverse mortgage loan until such time that the interest is paid.[9] Because the principal balance and the accrued interest on most reverse mortgages are expected to be repaid out of the proceeds from the sale of the borrower's residence securing the loan, when the borrower dies or moves out of his or her home, the foregoing rule is likely to significantly delay the date when reverse mortgage interest becomes deductible by most borrowers. This delay in the timing of deductions for reverse mortgage interest is likely to dramatically reduce their after-tax utility.

From the time-value-of-money perspective, deductions that are available to offset current taxable income yield greater after-tax economic benefit than deductions whose utility is realized over time. This is because when a deduction is immediately available, a taxpayer can invest the tax savings and earn investment income thereon. In contrast, when a deduction is postponed, the added earning potential of immediate tax savings is lost. In effect, when the time value of money is taken into account, the postponement of deductions for accrued reverse mortgage interest is equivalent to an interest-free loan to the United States government.

Even if one ignores time-value-of-money considerations, the delay in the deductibility of reverse mortgage interest may serve to eliminate the utility of the reverse mortgage interest deductions for many taxpayers. Given that the market for reverse mortgages consists primarily of elderly, retired individuals, it is entirely possible that at the time when a deduction for reverse mortgage interest becomes available the borrower (which may be the initial borrower's estate) simply may not have enough taxable income to absorb all of the interest deductions that accrued over the life of the loan.

SECURITIZATION OF REVERSE MORTGAGE LOANS VIA REMIC STRUCTURES

A Real Estate Mortgage Investment Conduit (REMIC) is a type of special-purpose entity that is commonly used to securitize mortgage loans and issue mortgage-backed securities to investors. The REMIC structure allows investors to receive allocated portions of interest on pools of mortgage assets held in a REMIC without incurring an extra layer of tax at the REMIC level. In general, REMICs are exempt from federal income tax. Furthermore, pass-through certificates issued by REMICs to investors (i.e., REMIC regular interests) are treated as debt instruments for U.S. federal income tax purposes.[10]

In order to qualify as a REMIC for U.S. federal income tax purposes, the special-purpose vehicle or asset pool used in a securitization is required to, among other things, make a REMIC election.[11] In addition, following the close of the third month beginning after its startup date, a REMIC must also maintain a static pool of assets consisting of "qualified mortgages" and other "permitted investments" (the "static asset pool test").[12] Until the REMIC rules were amended by Section 835 of the Jobs Act,[13] the static pool requirement effectively prevented REMICs from holding reverse mortgage loans. Because payments under reverse mortgage loans are considered separate loans that are contributed to a REMIC, under the prior version of the REMIC rules draws on reverse mortgage loans would have caused a REMIC to breach the static asset pool test.

The Jobs Act eliminated the foregoing issue by implementing several changes to the REMIC provisions. First, the Jobs Act modified the definition of the term *qualified mortgage*, by including in this definition not only reverse mortgage loans acquired at the startup of a REMIC, but also increases in the principal amount of reverse mortgage loans resulting from periodic advances made to the borrowers on such loans.[14] This change explicitly allows a REMIC to hold reverse mortgages, and to make periodic advances on such loans, without jeopardizing its REMIC status.

The Jobs Act did not add a definition of the term *reverse mortgage loan* to the Code. Instead, the definition of this term is contained in the legislative history of the Jobs Act. The legislative history defines the term *reverse mortgage loan* as a loan that: (1) is secured by an interest in real property; (2) provides for one or more advances of principal to the obligor, provided such advances are principally secured by an interest in the same real property as that which secures the loan; (3) may provide for a contingent payment at maturity based upon the value or appreciation in value of the real property securing the loan; (4) provides for an amount due at maturity that cannot exceed the value, or a specified fraction of the value, of the real property securing the loan; (5) provides that all payments under the loan are due only upon the maturity of the loan; and (6) matures after a fixed term or at the time the obligor ceases to use as a personal residence the real property securing the loan.[15]

Second, the Jobs Act included a change in the REMIC rules that allows REMIC regular interests to qualify even though the principal amount and/or the accrued interest may be reduced as a result of the nonoccurrence of one or more contingent payments with respect to reverse mortgage loans held by the REMIC, provided that on the startup day the REMIC sponsor "reasonably believed" that all principal and interest would be paid.[16] The legislative history to the Jobs Act specifies that the "reasonable belief" requirement would be met if the REMIC regular interest receives an investment-grade rating from at least one nationally recognized rating agency.[17] The intent of this change is to allow a reverse mortgage to be repaid from the proceeds of the sale of the residence securing the loan.

The other major reverse mortgage–related change to the REMIC provisions adopted by the Jobs Act involves the term *permitted investment*. The Jobs Act broadened the scope of permitted investments allowed to be held by a REMIC without violating the static asset pool test. Under the modified definition, a REMIC is permitted to maintain a "qualified reserve fund" consisting of intangible investment property to provide a source of funds for draws on pools of securitized reverse mortgage loans. However, such reserves are not permitted to exceed 50 percent of the fair market value of the assets held by a REMIC on its startup day (the "50 percent limit").[18]

The 50 percent limit could potentially become problematic for a REMIC if, as a result of the limitation, the reserve set aside by the REMIC proves to be insufficient to meet principal draws on its pool of reverse mortgages. This scenario could occur, for example, if draws on a REMIC's reverse mortgages turn out to be higher than expected because the borrowers exceed the mortality assumptions utilized in structuring the REMIC, or if voluntary prepayments of reverse mortgages are in excess of the expected rate.

To address the foregoing scenario, sponsors may need to retain residual interests in a reverse mortgage REMIC and contribute funds to the REMIC when its reserves are depleted due to unanticipated draws on the REMIC's reverse mortgages. Pursuant to the REMIC rules, holders of a residual interest in a REMIC are permitted to make contributions to a qualified reserve fund maintained by the REMIC following the startup date.[19] Contributions of assets to a REMIC following the startup date are otherwise generally subject to a punitive tax equal to 100 percent of the amount contributed.[20]

PRACTICAL OBSERVATIONS REGARDING INVESTMENT REVERSE MORTGAGE REMIC SECURITIES

Reverse mortgage REMIC securities raise some unique considerations for investors. For example, unlike in the case of REMICs securitized using traditional mortgages, payments of principal and interest on regular interests in reverse mortgage REMICs will be affected by the actual mortality rates experienced by the borrowers. For this reason, investors in reverse mortgage REMIC regular interests should base their investment decisions on their expectations regarding borrower mortality, in addition to prepayment rates and other factors.[21]

SUMMARY

Reverse mortgage loans are treated differently for federal income tax purposes from traditional residential mortgages. In the case of a typical reverse mortgage loan where the borrower is an individual and the repayment of the loan is secured by such borrower's personal residence, the loan would be considered "home equity indebtedness" and interest would be deductible at a maximum only on up to $100,000 of the principal balance of the loan. Furthermore, the deduction for interest would be deferred for taxpayers who use the cash receipts and disbursements method of accounting for tax purposes (i.e., most taxpayers who are individuals) until the interest is paid. These limitations are likely to greatly limit the utility of reverse mortgage interest deductions for many taxpayers.

In addition to restrictions on the deductibility of interest, reverse mortgage loans are subject to special rules governing their use in REMIC securitizations. Unlike traditional mortgage loans, reverse mortgage loans could not be used in REMIC securitizations until fairly recently. Modifications to the REMIC regime that permit the use of reverse mortgage loans in REMIC securitizations became effective for taxable years beginning after January 1, 2005. These rules contemplate that reverse mortgage REMICs may need to set up special reserves to fund draws on reverse mortgage loans held by such REMICs. Yields on REMIC securities backed by reverse mortgages may be especially affected by borrower mortality rates. Accordingly, prospective investors in reverse mortgage REMICs should base their investment decisions on expectations regarding borrower mortality rates, in addition to other, more traditional factors.

BHUYAN'S FINAL POINTS

- Understanding what tax implications a borrower may face could drive which loan products are successfully received by the marketplace and which are not.

> ■ The tax treatment for reverse mortgage lenders, and conse-
> quently investors in reverse mortgage–backed securities, will
> also drive the growth of this asset class. It is important to note
> once again that the timing of payments in a reverse mortgage
> investment are not predetermined, so the similarities between
> traditional mortgage–backed securities and reverse mortgages
> are limited.

NOTES

1. Code Sections 163(h)(2)(D) and 163(h)(3)(A).
2. Code Section 163(h)(3)(B).
3. Code Section 163(h)(3)(C).
4. Code Section 163(h)(4).
5. However, see 74 Fed. Reg. 66655 (Dec. 16, 2009), n. 2 ("The Federal Housing Administration (FHA) has announced a program that would enable eligible borrowers to use the proceeds of a federally-insured reverse mortgage for the purchase of a new principal residence. See U.S. Department of Housing and Urban Development (HUD) Mortgagee Letter 2008–23 (October 20, 2008) and HUD Mortgagee Letter 2009–11 (March 27, 2009).").
6. Code Section 163(h)(3)(B)(ii).
7. Code Section 163(h)(3)(C)(i) and (ii).
8. Under the cash receipts and disbursements method of accounting, amounts representing allowable deductions and items of gross income are, as a general rule, taken into federal income tax purposes for the taxable year in which they are paid or received, respectively. See Treasury Regulation Section 1.461-1(a)(1).
9. Rev. Rul. 80-248, 1980-2 C.B. 164 (Sept. 15, 1980); see also Code Section 1275(b)(2).
10. Code Section 860A.
11. Code Section 860D(a)(1).
12. Code Section 860D(a)(4).
13. The changes to the REMIC rules adopted under the Jobs Act became effective January 1, 2005.
14. Code Section 860G(a)(3).
15. H.R. Conf. Rep. No. 108-755, ¶ 11,180 (2004).
16. Section 835(b)(5)(A) of the Jobs Act; Code Section 860G(a)(1).
17. H.R. Conf. Rep. No. 108-755, ¶ 11,180 (2004).
18. Section 835(b)(8)(B) of the Jobs Act; Code Section 860G(a)(7).
19. Code Section 860(G)(d)(2)(D).

20. Code Section 860G(d)(1).

21. See e.g., Offering Circular Supplement, dated November 20, 2009, for Guaranteed HECM MBS REI Pass-Through Securities, Ginnie Mae REMIC Trust 2009-H01, p. S-6, available at http://structuredginniemaes.ginnienet.com/remicdb/deal/2009/001/GNMA-2009-001O-@OCS.PDF.

PART Four

Reverse Mortgages in Context

CHAPTER 10

Unlocking Housing Equity in Japan

Olivia S. Mitchell
Insurance & Risk Management, The Wharton School, University of Pennsylvania

John Piggott
School of Economics, University of New South Wales

Japan's aging rate is uniquely high among the developed countries. The explanation rests on Japan having experienced a shorter period of high fertility following World War II than other Organization for Economic Co-Operation and Development OECD economies. Births per family fell from 4.5 per family in 1947, to 2.7 in 1953, and to just 2 in 1957.[1] Australia, by contrast, had a fertility rate greater than 3 for all years between 1947 and 1961.[2] In Japan, the result has been a rapidly increasing dependency ratio, which in 2030 is predicted to be more than double the 1990 ratio of 21.6 percent. Some initial social security reforms have been recently enacted in Japan, and others proposed, including raising the eligibility age for the standard pension; nevertheless, projections suggest that these are not yet substantial enough to mitigate the expected cost explosion in public pensions as a result of demographic aging.[3]

The high value of residential real estate is another notable Japanese characteristic. An *Economist* survey recently showed that Tokyo and Osaka's residential property prices are the second most expensive of all western cities: An average two-bedroom city apartment in 2002 cost over 800,000.[4] More important, these real estate prices are high relative to Japanese average disposable incomes: Housing wealth as a proportion of annual disposable income in 1998 was 381 percent in Japan, the highest of all developed countries. The second highest, in Australia, was 355 percent, and the U.S. rate was a much smaller—163 percent.[5] Taken together, these facts indicate that the ability to use housing equity to supplement retirement income might be both timely, offering a partial solution to mounting public pension liabilities, and highly practicable. Reverse mortgages (*RMs*) can facilitate this process.

Yet establishing an RM tradition in Japan will not be easy. Simply making the Japanese people aware of RMs will not produce a viable market, because a strong financial infrastructure is required to insure the success of these products. In short, there must be safeguards for borrowers against unscrupulous lenders; there must be insurance available for lenders, who otherwise might not involve themselves with what are inherently risky contracts; and there must be a secondary market for reverse mortgages so that lenders have the option of selling some proportion of their RMs to other parties and thus avoid the high risk charges that accompany mortgages in general.[6] A thorough understanding of the riskiness of RMs and the appropriate level and cost of their insurance in the Japanese context is necessary to facilitate a Japanese RM market.

Furthermore, Japan has experienced a very long recession, falling property prices, and extremely low interest rates. Each of these facts will impinge upon the likely success of RMs. The latter two circumstances in particular will reduce the amount of money that households can borrow in relation to their property's value, while the first will promote a lack of confidence generally and diminish the appeal of little-known financial products. Nevertheless, RMs, properly implemented, do offer Japan a sound mechanism by which it can increase the consumption of its elderly and in the long term even reduce its public pension liabilities and healthcare costs. These considerations underscore the practical importance of this study.

The remainder of this chapter deals with the above issues in more detail, and where appropriate, compares the Japanese situation to those of other developed countries.

IMPLEMENTATION IN THE JAPANESE CONTEXT

To determine where and why RMs would work well in the future and for whom, we next explore conditions supportive of, and detrimental to, the process of unlocking home equity for elderly homeowners. We begin by focusing on general conditions, and then we turn to some specific conditions that may be particularly relevant to Japan.

Conditions Supportive of Unlocking Home Equity

As mentioned earlier, implementing the RM model for the elderly requires the lender to assemble several key pieces of information regarding the homes and their owners:

- Accurate initial home values, net of remaining mortgage and repairs to bring the property to code or zoning standards.
- Estimated transaction and closing costs, as well as expected servicing costs.
- Accurate forecasts of expected future home appreciation rates, taking into account adverse selection and/or moral hazard on the part of the borrowers.
- Accurate forecasts of residents' future expected mortality and termination patterns.
- Accurate forecasts of future expected riskless rates, mortgage rates, and annuity rates of return.
- Accurate forecasts of future tax/transfer policy, which influence the net costs and benefits of the RM options.

Clearly, these data demands are substantial, and even after more than a decade of experience in the United States, much remains to be learned to enhance the workings of the RM market.[7] On the positive side, U.S. housing markets operate relatively transparently and it is possible to obtain up-to-date house price series at the national and regional levels as illustrated above. Housing experts have also produced price indexes for specific cities over time, though a time series for a specific house or set of houses is, of course, more difficult to obtain. Nevertheless, the data tends to exist and is being collected since home sale information is generally a matter of public record and is increasingly being listed on the Internet. This may help in the development of forecasts for future home appreciation, though there exists a reasonably high level of price inertia in the U.S. market.[8] In general, lenders would probably demand insurance against the vagaries of the housing cycle, or diversify accordingly, so as to protect against the risk of housing market crashes such as those that have been noted in earlier chapters.

Less easy to obtain is information on likely transaction, closing, and servicing costs for RMs, though past experience probably provides a decent guide in the U.S. case. Little analysis has been done on the question of whether mortality and loan termination patterns are consistent with the underlying assumptions, and more should be done on this. Ultimately lenders would probably prefer protection against some massive change in mortality risk (e.g., a cure for cancer), but to date this is probably not diversifiable by private insurers.

Least easily predictable of all, probably, are future interest rates (including the riskless rate, mortgage rate, and rate used to price annuities) and future tax/transfer policies. In financial terms, the most critical issue is probably whether lenders can appropriately diversify their book of RM business, either by spreading investment pools geographically, by selling off their RMs in a secondary mortgage market, or by buying reasonably priced insurance to protect against key uncertainties. Some have argued that the private market can securitize reverse mortgages, though the U.S. market has not developed particularly rapidly. This is in part because RMs require monthly servicing and periodic credit reevaluations, requiring expensive and ongoing oversight. Life insurers might be thought to be natural entities that would buy these loans, since the life insurers take in cash up front and pay out later in life, while RM providers have the opposite cash flow pattern.[9] In general, however, an RM lender requires up-front liquidity given the nature of the product, since the loan or the annuity is paid immediately, but the house sale may be deferred long into the future.

Potential Payoffs of Reverse Mortgages in Japan

To illustrate the value of unlocking home equity in the international context, we use the model developed above to evaluate loan balance and annuity payments under alternative reverse mortgage scenarios. Table 10.1 illustrates possible payouts for two home equity levels, $100,000 and $300,000, values that bracket illustrative elderly homeowners' equity values in the United States and Japan, respectively.

We focus mainly on the results for age 85 here, though for completeness the tables show results for ages 65 and 75 as well. Our computations employ economic assumptions relevant to each country, regarding the inflation rate and the riskless real rate of return, as well as real annuity and mortgage rates.[10] These represent rather different economic conditions, with Japan assumed to experience deflation and negative real home equity growth (RG), as has been the case for several years; by contrast, the U.S. simulation assumes low but positive price inflation and real home equity growth. We use country-specific mortality data, namely period population mortality tables for U.S. females provided by the Office of the Chief Actuary of the Social Security Administration and data for Japanese females from the JLT18 mortality tables.[11] Finally, for this experiment, we presume that lenders would charge the same real loan rate (RM) on the reverse mortgage in both countries.

TABLE 10.1   Value of Home Equity

Payment Option	Age	United States		Japan	
		$100K	$300K	$100K	$300K
I. Lump sum	65	53,635	160,905	39,871	119,613
	75	66,623	199,869	54,579	163,737
	85	79,281	237,843	70,078	210,234
II. Real annuity	65	3,713	11,139	1,807	5,421
	75	6,489	19,467	3,711	11,133
	85	12,584	37,752	8,087	24,261

Notes: Authors' computations assume initial home equity set (respectively) of $100,000 and $300,000 for loan taken out by female at given age, surviving according to (respectively) Japanese or U.S. population tables.
A. U.S. economic assumptions: Risk-free real rate $(r) = 2.0\%$; Real home equity growth rate $(r + g) = 1.0\%$; Real mortgage rate $(r + m) = 4.5\%$; Real AIR for annuity $(r + a) = 3.0\%$.
B. Japan economic assumptions: Risk-free real rate $(r) = -0.6\%$; Real home equity growth rate $(r + g) = -2.4\%$; Real mortgage rate $(r + m) = 1.9\%$; Real AIR for annuity $(r + a) = 0.4\%$.

The simulation model generates a range of outputs for reverse mortgage potential payouts.[12] The first panel of Table 10.1 indicates that an 85-year-old in the United States would, under this formulation, be eligible to borrow a lump sum of approximately $238,000 against her home equity of $300,000. Longer Japanese life expectancies combined with less favorable projected rates of home equity growth imply that an 85-year-old Japanese woman would anticipate receiving a lump sum 12 percent lower, around $210,000. The second panel shows the real annuity that the 85-year-old woman could anticipate. For the U.S. case, the woman would expect an annual real benefit stream of almost $38,000 per year over her remaining lifetime. By contrast, under Japanese assumptions, the woman could anticipate a real flow of $24,300 annually, or one-third less than in the U.S. case. On these grounds, it might be reasonable to conclude that the lump sum approach to reverse mortgages might be more strongly preferred in Japan versus the United States, as compared to the annuity approach, since the lump sum offers a relatively larger bite of the home equity value. Nevertheless, it is worth noting that an elderly Japanese woman receiving a real lifetime annuity of over $24,000 would have a replacement rate of almost 60 percent, assuming average income for retired households.[13]

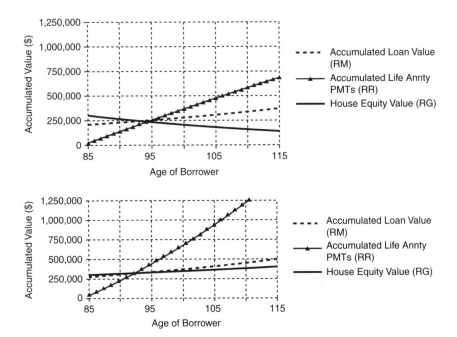

FIGURE 10.1   Lifetime Profile of Assets versus Liabilities in a Reverse Mortgage Setting

Two alternative scenarios, assuming borrower with $300,000 in home equity. Japanese female, age 85 at loan date, (a) Japanese economic assumptions, and (b) U.S. economics assumptions.

Notes: The following economic assumptions were employed: (a) Inflation rate = −0.6% annually (2001 estimate; www.cia.gov/cia/publications/factbook/fields/2092.html). r = −1.2 − (−0.6) = −0.6% (last 12 most as of October 2000: www.boj.or.jp/en/siryo/sk/ske4.pdf), r + a = −0.6 + 1 = 0.4%, r + g = −3 − (−0.6) = −2.4% (www.boj.or.jp/en/siryo/sk/ske4.pdf), r + m = 2.5 + (−0.6) = 1.9%. (b) Inflation rate = 1.5% (last 12 most as of December 2000; www.econedlink.org/lessons/index.cfm?lesson=EM222). r = 3.5 − 1.5 = 2% (one-year Treasury rate December 2002; www. federalreserve.gov/releases/h15/data/a/tcmly.txt), r + a = 2 + 1 = 3%, r + g = 1%, r + m = 2 + 2.5 = 4.5% (YES).

A different way to visualize the output of this model is to graph the expected patterns by age, comparing real home appreciation (or depreciation), and the growth rate of the loan under a reverse mortgage. This is provided in Figure 10.1, assuming two different scenarios. Panel A posits an 85-year-old Japanese female along with all the "Japanese case" assumptions, while panel B uses female Japanese mortality tables but posits more optimistic assumptions consistent with the "U.S. economic scenario."

Results are given for both a lump sum and an annuity payout profile for the reverse mortgage.

Both cases assume that the homeowner has initial home equity worth $300,000 and applies for the loan at age 85. Under assumptions relevant to Japan over the past decade, represented in the top panel, the home's value sinks in real terms over time. If the reverse mortgage were taken as a lump sum, the loan would initially be worth about $210,000.

If the borrower reached age 90, the cumulative loan plus interest would grow to roughly $231,000, and by age 95, the loan would be worth on the order of $254,000. If, instead, the borrower took an annuity payment option, her loan value would be initially about $24,000, growing to $141,000 conditional on survival to age 90, and to $254,000 by age 95. Under the Japanese economic assumptions the loan balance crosses over, or equals the home equity, at around age 95. It is interesting that the age of crossover is virtually identical for both the lump sum and the annuity payout approach. Of course, the size of the shortfall is higher in the lump sum case than in the annuity case, since the payout is more gradual with the annuity. Further, the shortfall rises with the mortgage loan rate and the annuity interest rate, and falls with the rate of appreciation expected on the home, all else equal.[14]

The second scenario uses Japanese mortality tables but the more optimistic U.S economic forecasts. Not surprisingly, the projected growth in home equity permits a higher initial lump sum loan, of about $226,000, which grows to $281,000 by age 90, and $350,000 by age 95, conditional on survival. The starting annuity is also higher, almost $30,000 per year, growing to $188,000 and $360,000 5 and 10 years out. It is interesting that the crossover age in scenarios A and B are about the same, age 95, despite the different economic assumptions. In other words, RM lenders in the Japan market would worry about "crossover risk" just as in the United States. The larger size of the loans under the U.S. assumptions, however, mean that the size of the potential shortfall as modeled here would be greater than under the more conservative Japanese economic assumptions.

FEASIBILITY OF REVERSE MORTGAGES IN JAPAN

Inasmuch as the evidence suggests that older Japanese homeowners could substantially enhance their consumption with reverse mortgages, we next explore what factors might facilitate the development of these products in the Japanese context. We identify two types of issues that must be addressed in this discussion, first those having to do with the housing market, and second, those having to do with the financial market more generally.

One serious problem confronting the Japanese housing market, and an issue that especially challenges the RM market, is the low volume of trades in established housing. This is a problem since the development of RMs requires accurate home valuation methodologies and data. Yet information on housing trades in Japan is sparse, partly because few elderly move.[15] Some argue that the lack of information regarding housing values and housing trades has directly impeded the development of RMs in Japan. Unlike in the United States, Japanese realtors appear to provide very little information to the public on housing quality and housing market values. Indeed, outside of commercial property, there appear to be no real estate indexes available.[16] Such information asymmetry makes it extremely difficult for borrowers as well as lenders to develop accurate forecasts of future returns (and volatility) for housing values. Lack of standard property pricing data also deters the development of a secondary market for reverse mortgages, which earlier we have argued could make much more liquid the market for housing equity.

A related concern is that a well-functioning housing market requires high-quality credit information on potential borrowers, which also may be less widespread in Japan as compared to more financially integrated economies. For example, U.S. credit bureaus readily provide very low-cost credit ratings to actual and potential customers, whereas in Japan this is not as common. Perhaps the discrepancy may explain why such a high fraction of a home's purchase price is required in Japan as a down payment, typically 30–50 percent of the purchase price of the property, versus 10 percent or less in the United States,[17] perhaps because high down-payment rates result from the Japan Housing Lending Corporation's approach as the main mortgage lender in the country, financed mainly from the postal savings system and mostly dedicated to new homes (fewer than 10% of the loan volume goes to existing homes). Furthermore, home loans from this source total only 30–40 percent of the house and lot value, another obstacle to building equity in the first place.

Research by Flavin and Yamashita (2002)[18] in the U.S. context demonstrates that high down payments and closing costs constrain the housing market; an international survey by Chiuri and Jappelli (2000)[19] also finds that higher down payments are associated with lower owner-occupancy rates for housing. In practice, high-quality credit information is less valuable in the case of reverse mortgages, since the nonrecourse nature of the home loan means that homeowner credit histories are not as crucial as in the case of regular, forward mortgages. Nevertheless, credit histories are being used as an indicator of timeliness in paying hazard insurance bills and a wide variety of other consumer behavior, so an underdeveloped credit market could pose a problem for the growth of the RM market as well.

Even if the supply of reverse mortgages were to be developed in Japan, there remains a question as to whether Japanese elders would demand them. That is, how many would borrow against their housing equity to fund old-age consumption? Some research would imply that there might be little demand, since among households aged 65 and older, almost two-thirds indicate that they intend to leave a bequest, mainly via their house and land and averaging ¥66Mm[20] (Tachibanaki, 1994). On the other hand, one could argue that these expectations will be changing as life expectancies rise and incomes of the elderly are pared down to bring the old-age pension system closer to solvency. Nevertheless, tax regulations seem to promote property transfer by bequest rather than sale; thus Noguchi and Poterba (1994)[21] argue that property tax rules plus inheritance tax and the Land Lease Law greatly choke the supply of land and houses in Japan, and may drive the traditional Japanese co-residence tradition where adult children move in with their parents and provide an effective consumption annuity in exchange for the promise of the bequest of the property at the parents' death.

Offsetting these negative concerns are two positive sets of evidence that may indicate the feasibility of Japanese reverse mortgage markets. First, Goetzmann and Spiegel (2000)[22] have recently shown that housing has dominated as an investment asset in most nations, since other assets provide higher returns for lower risk. As a consequence, they recommend that governments everywhere must become far more cautious in encouraging housing investment among the "financially vulnerable," which would presumably include the house-rich, cash-poor elderly. Second, some encouraging evidence is provided by Kase (1994),[23] who explored an actual reverse mortgage program implemented in Musashino City, a suburb of Tokyo, in 1981. This publicly supported effort provided support services to the elderly in exchange for payment of a monthly bill, or a reimbursement amount taken from the homeowner's equity, where repayment was deferred until the sale of the person's property. The funds plus a 5 percent annual fixed interest rate could not exceed 80 percent of the value of the land (the government allocated no value to the building). Though this is clearly an early effort (only 42 people signed up for the reverse mortgage program), it illustrates that there may be some substantial demand on the part of the elderly, and some willingness on the part of governments to provide such products.

The growth and development of reverse mortgage markets in Japan also awaits better ways to forecast expected future home appreciation rates, taking into account adverse selection and/or moral hazard on the part of the borrowers; accurate forecasts of residents' future expected mortality and termination patterns; accurate forecasts of future expected riskless rates, mortgage rates, and annuity rates of return; and accurate forecasts of future tax/transfer policy, which influence the net costs and benefits of the RM options. This information set is clearly substantial though some progress can be made quickly, perhaps in the area of better mortality tables for annuitants as contrasted to population tables (McCarthy and Mitchell, in press).[24]

In the end, jump-starting the RM market in Japan would probably require a central government effort along several lines. Several U.S. institutions are supportive of reverse mortgages, including the Federal Housing Administration, which has provided federally backed reinsurance to support lenders that sell reverse mortgage products to the elderly. In addition, Fannie Mae and Freddie Mac have also supported these markets, with Fannie Mae purchasing virtually all the reverse mortgages on offer in the United States. Establishing similar institutions in Japan might afford certain advantages, since in the United States, these government-backed groups are widely credited with bringing securitization to the housing market (Szymanoski, 1999).[25] Yet it is unclear whether establishing new institutions such as these in Japan would be politically and economically feasible at present. The Japanese government already faces serious budget constraints, and taking on potentially massive new reinsurance liabilities would be very risky.

Even more politically difficult might be the fact reverse mortgage borrowers would have to have property appraisals conducted and the results provided to possible lenders. In that process, many elderly who had up to then experienced only "latent" capital losses would become aware just how much their properties had lost in value as a result of the decade-long recession. In turn, banks and other mortgage holders would have to recognize that the book value of many assets had declined precipitously, making their financial condition appear all the more precarious. In other words, making the RM market work in Japan would probably be supportive of other needed financial sector reforms, but these might not necessarily be politically palatable.

Experts see several valuable roles for government in this area. One is in eliminating regulatory and tax barriers limiting the products' development. For example, tax reform and clarification/unification of real estate laws would greatly enhance opportunities for profitability. Another factor that would greatly strengthen the operation of the market in Japan would be the building of a market database on housing quality, trades, and prices (Rasmussen et al., 1996; Nishimura and Shimizu, 2003).[26] In the U.S. case, this was necessary for Lehman Brothers to securitize the entire RM book of business for the Financial Freedom Senior Funding Corporation in 1999 (Rodda et al., 2000).[27] Another role for government was demonstrated in the U.S. case, where Fannie Mae offers the possibility that at least one investor provides liquidity for banks to take on the reverse mortgages.

DiPasquale and Wheaton (1996)[28] note that to launch a secondary market for regular (forward) mortgages in the United States, the mortgages had to be "commoditized," or standardized with similar terms. For instance, the mortgage had to be 30-year, fixed rate, and self-amortizing, and borrowers had to meet similar qualification standards (i.e., the monthly mortgage payment plus taxes and insurance initially had to be less than 28 percent of income to qualify for the loan). A parallel structure in Japan might be required to make RMs become feasible for the private lending market.

SUMMARY

Evidence suggests that many older Japanese have quite high levels of home equity, notwithstanding the recent decline in real estate prices in that nation. At the same time, Japanese life expectancy rates are also among the highest in the world. These long life spans, when paired with very low fertility, mean that the Japanese retirement systems face almost certain future insolvency. This report suggests that methods of unlocking home equity in Japan could be developed to boost consumption among the elderly, reduce public pension liability, and mitigate the demand for long-term care facilities. Creative ways to finance old-age consumption in Japan, by tapping home equity, might substantially improve retirement security in this rapidly aging country.

Previous literature on asset patterns by age has often overlooked housing wealth as a determinant of retiree wellbeing, particularly in the Japanese context. Here we have collected and analyzed a range of international data on housing wealth patterns by age. Evidence from the Japanese National Family Income and Expenditure Survey (NFIES), and other sources, indicates some similarities regarding levels and patterns of home equity by age across countries. There are also many financing mechanisms that could help unlock housing wealth for retirement consumption, and here we focus on the potential implications of reverse mortgages (RMs) in a comparative context. Using Japanese and U.S. mortality tables, as well as other economic assumptions, we compute the lump-sum values, as well as the real annuity payments, that could be financed under alternative RM schemes in the United States and Japan.

Our analysis suggests several conclusions. First, we show that Japan offers an environment conducive to the development, implementation, and encouragement of reverse mortgages. Japanese elderly today command relatively high levels of home equity by international standards. Consequently, this demographic group could expect substantial value from unlocking home equity with a reverse mortgage. In addition, the decline in Japanese fertility over the past 50 years implies that older households will have fewer children, implying that the elderly may curtail their supply of bequests to the next (smaller) generation. This should make it easier for the elderly to unlock home equity for consumption purposes during their lifetimes.

A second conclusion is that the use of reverse mortgages could alleviate some of the financial strain that population aging imposes on the Japanese economy and budget. Old-age pensions already face insolvency, and the new Japanese long-term care program portends additional budgetary pressures. Retirement incomes are typically below labor earnings in Japan, and stringencies imposed by financing problems are further depressing the benefit replacement rate that can be financed by the PAYGO social security system. This, too, is likely to have a positive impact on the demand for RMs.

Despite long Japanese life expectancy and less-than-robust economic conditions, we also conclude that Japanese elderly could experience a large income increase from a reverse annuity if it were paid out in a lump sum, or in the form of an annual income stream until death. Replacement rates might be boosted substantially with the development of an RM market that permitted older Japanese to finance consumption using their home equity.

Policymakers wanting to establish a market for reverse mortgages in Japan would have to mitigate several factors that appear to impede the development of such products. For one, tax and regulatory obstacles would need to be removed to support these financial arrangements. Exempting reverse mortgages from capital gains and transactions taxes would certainly make these financial products more appealing. Another area requiring attention has to do with the tax treatment of income from reverse mortgages: for instance, making annuity income flows from RMs tax exempt would likely enhance their appeal to the elderly. Tax policy is also crucial to lenders, who would be more likely to find the market viable if regulations permitted them to deduct interest payments accumulating on RMs but not payable until the sale of the house. The precise pattern of tax rules surrounding RMs would have to be considered in the context of the broader prevailing tax regime.

To help the elderly unlock their home equity, it would also be critical for Japan to develop a clear and transparent legal framework for reverse mortgage contracts. The borrower and the lender must understand clearly the obligations each takes on when making the deal, and each must have legal recourse in the event of fraud or misbehavior. For instance, U.S. lenders are forced to contend with real estate and insurance laws that differ across the 50 United States, making it impossible to have a standard, nationally enforceable RM contract. This complexity undermines the potential for scale economies and standardization on the part of the lenders, and it also makes it difficult to educate potential borrowers about the nature of the products. Undue complexity also gives rise to potential conflicts of interest between lenders and borrowers, once an individual loan has reached the crossover point.

Japanese housing markets would also need to be modernized in several ways if RMs are to function effectively in this nation. Enhanced information flows would be needed regarding sale prices and characteristics of both new and existing residential property.[29]

This would permit the securitization of housing loans and lines of credit, both of which we have argued make home equity accessible to older persons. Establishing reinsurance mechanisms would also encourage lenders to offer these products while offering them some protection against crossover risk. In the U.S. case, the federal government has played a key role in the development of standardized price and housing quality data via the two housing loan authorities, Fannie Mae and Freddie Mac. To develop the basic information required for securitization in Japan's housing market, it would likely be necessary to have the federal government jumpstart the process with a similar set of institutions. Transactions costs and servicing costs would also have to be kept down by competition and enhanced market fluidity, ideally to below rates currently charged in the United States (e.g., 6% of the initial loan value in the case of a lump-sum loan).

Policies supportive of RM markets would also include changes in other financial sectors complementary to the RM market. For example, strengthening the life insurance sector would make more appealing the sale of lifelong annuity streams, a key piece of the annuity-oriented version of the RM structure. Having a strong long-term bond market is also critical to the development of RM loans, since lenders would need to borrow long-term in order to pay out the lump sums and annual income flows needed by the elderly who wish to unlock their home equity. The recent move by the U.S. federal government to offer inflation-protected bonds is a key element in a long-term commitment to help preserve consumption streams of the elderly.

Implementing a program of RMs would be a fruitful means of helping the elderly finance their consumption in Japan, a particularly valuable development against the backdrop of financial stringencies facing the government. Of course additional modeling would be helpful, in order to develop a clearer idea of potential costs and benefits in the Japanese context. For example, our model along with others in the RM literature assumes a deterministic interest rate process; additional research is required incorporating sources of volatility and correlation across assets and liabilities. Our model also assumes no transaction costs, or conversely, that homeowners have substantial net equity after accounting for these costs; additional research would be useful on the likely level of such costs in Japan. Additional analysis would also be required to determine the value of lender insurance required in the Japanese context. Demand for such insurance will be greater when residential housing values are declining, and interest rates are low, which is apparently true for Japan in the near term. Further research would also be useful in exploring alternative ways to structure RM payments so as to make the products more appealing to borrowers, and how these might vary with key parameters of interest.

BHUYAN'S FINAL POINTS

- Japan's dire aging crisis and sluggish economy may be an ideal setting for the reverse mortgage product.
- The aging population in Japan is putting tremendous strain on retirement programs. Seniors may need to provide for the own retirements by way of reverse mortgages.
- Mobility rates in Japan are much lower than in the United States.
- Japanese seniors hold a substantial amount of home equity.
- It is important to consider the lack of Japanese actuarial data and the fact that Japanese life expectancies are among the highest in the world.
- A Japanese-specific product would need to be developed in order to increase its probability of success.

NOTES

1. This refers to the population aged 65+ as a proportion of the working-age population.
2. See the *Year Book Australia* 2002 (ABS, 2002).
3. R. Disney and P. Johnson, *Pension Systems and Retirement Incomes Across OECD Countries* (Edward Elgar, 2001), 16.
4. See *The Economist*, May 28, 2002.
5. L. Ellis and D. Andrews, "City Sizes, Housing Costs, and Wealth," research discussion paper, Reserve Bank of Australia, October 2001.
6. When lending institutions hold assets that are perceived as relatively risky, such as mortgages, regulatory agencies will insist that the institutions increase their proportion of capital to facilitate greater confidence in repayment. Thus lenders like to sell some proportion of their mortgages to avoid the associated capital charges. Indeed, the new Basel Capital Adequacy provisions of 1999 specifically emphasize the importance of risk weighting in relation to assets. The relative

riskiness of assets in institutions' portfolios is becoming a more important determinant of their capital requirements. This issue is therefore very relevant for RMs.

7. E. J. Szymanoski and T. R. DiVenti, "Demand and Supply Issues in RM Lending: The U.S. Experience and Its Implications for Eastern Europe and Russia," paper presented at the *International AREAUEA Conference*, Cancun, Mexico, May 2001.

8. R. J. Shiller and A. N. Weiss, "Home Equity Insurance," working paper DP 1074, Cowles Foundation, July 1994.

9. On the other hand, prior research has shown that life insurance and annuities are not necessarily a good hedge for each other; see McCarthy and Mitchell (in press).

10. For Japanese historical data, the following assumptions were employed: inflation rate $= -0.6\%$ annually (2001 estimate; www.cia.gov/cia/publications/factbook/fields/2092.html), $r = -1.2 - (-0.6) = -0.6\%$ (last 12 months as of October 2002: www.boj.or.jp/en/siryo/sk/ske4.pdf), $r + a = -0.6 + 1 = 0.4\%$, $r + g = -3 - (-0.6) = -2.4\%$ (www.boj.or.jp/en/siryo/sk/ske4.pdf), $r + m = 2.5 + (-0.6) = 1.9\%$ (same real rate assumed for United States and Japan). For the case consistent with U.S. assumptions, we used the following: inflation rate $= 1.5\%$ (last 12 months as of December 2002; www.econedlink.org/lessons/index.cfm?lesson=EM222), $r = 3.5 - 1.5 = 2\%$ (1-year Treasury rate December 2002; www.federalreserve.gov/releases/h15/data/a/tcm1y.txt), $r + a = 2 + 1 = 3\%$, $r + g = 1\%$ (as per Tom Davidoff), $r + m = 2 + 2.5 = 4.5\%$ (same real rate assumed for United States and Japan).

11. O. S. Mitchell, J. M. Poterba, M. Warshawsky, J. R. Brown, 1994. "New Evidence on the Money's Worth of Individual Annuities," *Amer. Econ. Rev.* 89 (December 1994): 1299–1318; and Ministry of Health and Welfare, "The 18th Life Tables," Statistics and Information Department, Minister's Secretariat, Tokyo, 1998.

12. To simplify computations, they assume no closing or servicing costs. Consequently, payouts are an upper bound as compared to results with such costs incorporated.

13. R. L. Clark and O. S. Mitchell, "Strengthening Employment-Based Pensions in Japan," *Benefits Quarterly* 2 (2002): 22–43.

14. It should be noted that these computations are deterministic, so they do not allow for volatility in any of the key rates, nor do we include correlations between the various rates. Studies of the HECM product do make simplifying assumptions about means, standard deviations, and correlations of key variables; see Szymanoski (1994).

15. T. Ishikawa and Y. Yajima, Savings, Consumption and Real Assets of the Elderly in Japan and the U.S.: How the Existing-Home Market Can Boost Consumption," working paper No. 149, NLI Research Institute, 2001.

16. For more discussion on this point, see Nishimura and Shimizu (2003).

17. M. Seko, "Housing in a Wealth-Based Economy: The Case of Japan," *Japanese Econ. Stud.* 22(2) (1994a): 65–92.

18. M. Flavin and T. Yamashita, "Owner-Occupied Housing and the Composition of the Household Portfolio," *Amer. Econ. Rev.* (March 2002): 345–362.

19. M. C. Chiuri and T. Jappelli, "Financial Market Imperfections and Home Ownership: A Comparative Study," 2000.

20. T. Tachibanaki, "Housing and Saving in Japan," in Yukio Noguchi and J. Poterba (Eds.), *Housing Markets in the United States and Japan* (Chicago: University of Chicago Press, 1994), 161–189.

21. Y. Noguchi and J. Poterba, "Introduction," in *Housing Markets in the United States and Japan* (Chicago: University of Chicago Press), pp. 1–10.

22. W. Goetzmann and M. Spiegel, "The Policy Implications of Portfolio Choice in Underserved Mortgage Markets," working paper 00-18, Yale Center for Finance, October 2000.

23. H. Kase, "Case Management in Home Care Service in Japan," in H. G. Stopp Jr. (Ed.), *International Perspectives on Healthcare for the Elderly* (New York: Peter Lang, 1994), 91–96.

24. D. McCarthy and O. S. Mitchell, "International Adverse Selection in Life Insurance and Annuities," in S. Tuljapurkar (Ed.), *Population Aging in the Industrialized Countries: Challenges and Explorations,* in press.

25. E. Szymanoski, "Risk and the Home Equity Conversion Mortgage," *J. Amer. Real Estate Urban Econ. Assoc.* 22(2) (1994): 347–366.

26. D. Rasmussen, I. Megbolubge, and P. A. Simmons, "The Reverse Mortgage as an Instrument for Lifetime Financial Planning: An Analysis of Market Potential," Fannie Mae Foundation research report, Washington, D.C., November 1996; and K. Nishimura and C. Shimizu, "Distortion in Land Price Information: Mechanism in Sales Comparables and Appraisal Value Relation," discussion paper, University of Tokyo, Tokyo, 2003.

27. D. T. Rodda, C. Herbert, and H.-K. Lam (Ken), "Evaluation Report of FHA's Home Equity Conversion Mortgage Insurance Demonstration," Contract No. DU100C000005978, Task Order 12, Final Report to HUD, March 2000.

28. D. DiPasquale and W. C. Wheaton, *Urban Economics and Real Estate Markets* (Englewood Cliffs, NJ: Prentice Hall International, 1996).

29. Nishimura and Shimizu (2003) discuss information shortfalls in the Japanese property market.

CHAPTER 11

The Secondary Market in Home Equity Conversion Mortgages

Charles A. Stone
Brooklyn College, City University of New York

Anne Zissu
Citytech, City University of New York, Polytechnic University

H ome equity is an important asset class. For senior citizens the importance of this asset class is magnified by the income constraints many seniors face. Reverse mortgages offer seniors a way of liquidating the equity of their homes without increasing periodic expenditures that accompany increased leverage. The reverse mortgage in general and the Home Equity Conversion Mortgage (HECM) in particular, which is the focus of this chapter, allow seniors to issue debt against a portion of their home equity. The credit drawn against the home equity using the HECM amounts to a series of secured zero-coupon bonds against the equity in their home.

THE REVERSE MORTGAGE TO LIQUIDATE HOME EQUITY

The decision about how resources should flow between generations is complex. We do not address the choice of leaving wealth to heirs or having heirs protect their inheritance by substituting private transactions for market transactions. In this chapter our discussion is a brief description of the HECM, the HMBS, and the HMBS REMIC. The Home Equity Conversion Mortgage (HECM) was introduced by HUD in 1989 as a pilot program and became permanent in 1998 (Evaluation Report of FHA's Home Equity

Conversion Mortgage Insurance Demonstration Contract No. DU100C000005978, Task Order No. 12, Final Report, March 31, 2000, *prepared for* Edward J. Szymanoski, U.S. Department of Housing and Urban Development, 451 Seventh Street, SW, Room 8212, Washington, D.C. 20410-3000; *prepared by* David T. Rodda Christopher Herbert Hin-Kin (Ken) Lam.)

The market is relatively small but has the potential to serve a growing segment of the population—seniors who have income constraints and who have accumulated wealth in the form of home equity and who prefer to remain in their current homes rather than moving.

HECM is the dominant reverse mortgage contract that is issued in the United States. It is estimated that HECMs comprise 90 percent of the stock of reverse mortgages in the United States and the current flow of reverse mortgages will likely support this percentage.

The HECM is becoming more liquid, at a time when liquidity is at a premium, due to GNMA's development of the HMBS, which is a guaranteed pass-through security backed by HECMs. Ginnie Mae refers to data that forecasts a 25 to 30 percent growth in HECM originations. The demographic drivers that GNMA cites for increased origination volume are 80 percent homeownership of the 65-and-older population that will number 35 million by 2010 and 50 million by 2020. Ginnie Mae is using HMBSs as collateral used in *real estate mortgage conduits*. REMICs used to finance pools of HECMs will enable the risks and benefits of HECM portfolios to be more efficiently distributed. While securitization has been much maligned since the private markets for MBSs collapsed in 2007, securitization is still the way to expand the capital base available to finance pools of illiquid financial instruments such as reverse mortgages. The language of financial institutions regarding how the secondary market is used is quite similar to the language used to describe how conventional mortgages are refinanced.

According to the GNMA report to Congress, "Continued investor interest in Ginnie Mae's reverse-mortgage HECM securities helped to grow the HECM/HMBS portfolio in FY 2009. The unpaid principal balance of HMBS climbed to $6.1 billion and the number of participations (the funded portions of HECM loans that have been securitized) increased to 62,871, with more than 42 percent of this participation volume occurring in the fourth quarter of FY 2009 alone. This has meant more liquidity, which translates into better execution and, ultimately, lower costs for the growing elderly population" (Ginnie Mae Report to Congress Fiscal Year 2009, November 6, 2009, U.S. Department of Housing and Urban Development).

Figure 11.1 shows the growth in terms of the initial principal limit of the loans originated. Figure 11.2 illustrates the rapid increase in the rate of

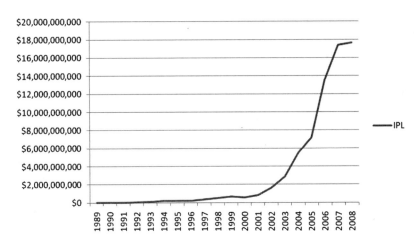

FIGURE 11.1   Initial Principal Limits by Year

growth in the HECM market when measured by the number of loans. It appears that the bubble in home values was recognized by a group of borrowers or perhaps by the lenders, who signaled that it was time to cash in on the inflated home equity values by originating HECMs. The *initial principal limit (IPL)* is the gross amount available by issuing an HECM.

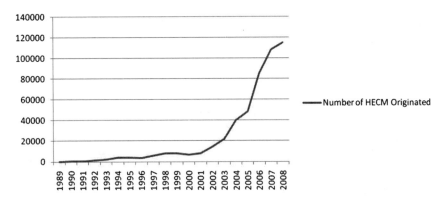

FIGURE 11.2   Number of HECMs Originated
Source: Tables from HUD, www.hud.gov/offices/hsg/comp/rpts/hecmsfsnap/hecmsfsnap.cfm.

HECM: A FINANCIAL INNOVATION

The HECM is a financial innovation that meets the needs of senior citizens who do not have sufficient income to cover current and/or expected future expenditures and continue to live in the homes they own. HECMs offer senior citizens a way to liquidate their home equity wealth without having to sell their homes and without creating a current obligation. The HECM enables senior citizens to expand their periodic consumption to a greater extent than a forward mortgage because the HECM contract does not require any repayment of interest or principal until a maturity event occurs. Forward mortgages and reverse mortgages are not substitutes. The forward mortgage can support a larger debt/equity ratio because it is designed to amortize over time, has a firm maturity date, and underwriting standards are based on covering payments with a multiple of income. A forward mortgage is designed to create a growth in home equity through amortization. This offers a layer of protection to the lender when the initial loan-to-value ratio is sized correctly. The 30-year fixed-rate mortgage is suitable for financing property that has value in excess of what one can currently afford based on accumulated savings. The reverse mortgage is suitable for tapping into an accumulated source of wealth to supplement other sources of income.

A reverse mortgage offers senior citizens a means of liquidating one form of current wealth (home equity) without actually being forced to sell the asset. In the case of housing, this is very important because people derive satisfaction and wellbeing from being able to live in their homes. Seniors who have accumulated wealth in the form of diversified portfolios of financial assets will liquidate these to supplement income. Selling shares in an IRA is not as disruptive as selling a home. For seniors who have been able to accumulate sufficient wealth for retirement, liquidating financial assets will be the first choice to supplement income; for those who have not accumulated sufficient wealth in financial assets, real assets can become an important source of income. The primary real asset that has a viable market and that is widely held in sufficient amounts to enable people to maintain the current standards of living is home equity. Whereas the HECM will not give people the same amount of cash as a home sale, it does afford them the opportunity to live in their home for as long as they choose to do so.

Recently it became possible for seniors to use the HECM to finance the purchase of a property as well as simply to liquidate home equity (October 20, 2008, Mortgagee Letter 2008-33, To: All Approved Mortgagees, All Hud-Approved Housing Counseling Agencies; Subject: Home Equity Conversion Mortgage (HECM) for Purchase Program, from FHA and signed by Brian D. Montgomery, Assistant Secretary for Housing-Federal Housing Commissioner).

This is useful for a homeowner who has a home that may be too large or in the wrong location. By selling their current home and issuing a reverse mortgage to finance the new home, buyers can reinvest all or part of the sale proceeds in a new home and leverage the new home with a reserve mortgage. Issuing an HECM instead of a forward mortgage expands rather than constrains current consumption possibilities. The HECM offers to households the benefits of the zero-coupon-bond structure that companies and governments enjoy.

CASH FLOWS, RISK, AND UNCERTAINTY

The uncertainty that drives a yield wedge between Treasury bonds and GNMA-guaranteed MBSs is prepayment risk. Mortgagors can prepay all or part of their mortgage debt at any time between origination and maturity. This makes the timing of principal cash flows and the magnitude of interest cash flows uncertain. Reverse mortgagors can also choose to prepay their HECMs, but the main element that investors in reverse mortgages discount is longevity risk. In the case of HECMs, it is tenure and longevity risks that make the HECM both a difficult and a potentially valuable instrument to manage. A maturity event is triggered when the mortgaged home ceases to be the primary residence of the mortgagor or tax and insurance liabilities accumulate against the property. Mortgagors who have issued HECMs are obligated to keep taxes and insurance current. The HECM also requires that the mortgagor maintains his or her property. Maintenance of the property's value is critical since it is the value of the property upon which the lender's loan and guarantor's guarantee are secured. Both the forward and reverse mortgages expose lenders and guarantors to the risk that the value of the mortgaged property will fall below the loan balance plus accrued interest. This risk is greater for the reverse mortgage because the loan does not amortize. In both cases price risk is limited by requiring a layer of equity between the creditor/guarantor and the borrower. Sizing this equity layer so that it offers adequate protection without being overly constraining to borrowers is at the crux of the cause of the housing bubble and the future recovery in housing prices.

An asset that has negative cash flows for an uncertain number of periods with a return of principal and accrued interest at the uncertain maturity date is not an easy portfolio to finance or to manage. The difficulty in funding HECMs will be compounded if the portfolio is not large enough to perform as expected. In other words, if the portfolio of HECMs a bank owns is too small in numbers, then the risk and return will not be predictable within an acceptable range. Financial institutions that own only small, concentrated portfolios of HECMs would have to allocate excessive capital to support the asset class. Until 2009, FNMA was the buyer of first, last, and only resort for HECMs. A broad secondary market in HECMs does not yet exist, but it is quickly developing. FNMA is backing away from the market as the secondary market develops. At the core of this market is the *GNMA HECM mortgage-backed security (HMBS)*. GNMA does not buy pools of HECMs; rather GNMA guarantees the performance of the HMBS. Investors will receive the payment of accrued interest and principal when it is due.

FNMA has been the largest investor in HECMs. As of 2008, FNMA owned 90 percent of the outstanding market in HECMs. This would be considered a corner in most markets. It would certainly not qualify as a competitive market. By 2009, the share of the HECM market owned by FNMA had fallen to 50 percent. In terms of unpaid principal balance, the amount of FNMA's HECM portfolio was $50.2 billion as of December 31, 2009 (FNMA 10-K, 2009):

> *The outstanding unpaid principal balance of reverse mortgages included in our mortgage portfolio was $50.2 billion as of December 31, 2009 and $41.6 billion as of December 31, 2008. The majority of these loans are Home Equity Conversion Mortgages, a type of reverse mortgage product that has been in existence since 1989 and accounts for approximately 90 percent of the total market share of reverse mortgages. Our market share of new reverse mortgage acquisitions was approximately 90 percent in 2008 and 50 percent in 2009. The decrease in our market share was a result of the changes in our pricing strategy and market conditions and also resulted in our market share of acquisitions in the fourth quarter to fall below 10 percent. Because Home Equity Conversion Mortgages are insured by the federal government through the FHA, we believe that we have limited exposure to losses on these loans, although home price declines and a weak housing market have also affected the performance of this book.*

THE SECONDARY MARKET FOR HECM

The following excerpt illustrates the connection between originators of HECM and FNMA:

> *Next Generation Financial Services ("NGFS"), a division of the Bank, engages in the origination of reverse and conventional*

mortgage loans, providing these products directly through commission based loan officers throughout the United States. NGFS originates reverse mortgage loans for sale and currently sells all of its volume into the secondary market. The Bank does not originate any reverse mortgage loans for its portfolio, but it does retain the servicing rights on reverse mortgage loans sold to Fannie Mae. NGFS is one of the largest originators of reverse mortgage loans in the United States.

In 2006, GNMA introduced an HMBS that will be the foundation for a more liquid secondary market in HECMs. HECMs are being securitized, that is, securities are being issued backed by pools of HECMs. There have been a number of issues to date.

The model for the HMBS is the very successful GNMA MBS programs. HMBSs will be issued under the Ginnie Mae II Custom Program. When lenders securitize mortgages that conform to GNMA underwriting standards, the cash flows from amortizing mortgages are passed through to investors. GNMA controls the underwriting of mortgages that it is willing to allow into securitized pools that it guarantees. The GNMA guarantee assures that investors will receive the timely payment of interest and principal. Investors do not discount GNMA MBSs for credit risk. The risk to investors is derived from changes in interest rates and variations in mortgage prepayment.

Ginnie Mae is using its experience and success in the market for securitized FHA-guaranteed MBSs that are backed by forward mortgages to develop a standardized and liquid market in MBSs backed by HECMs.

The most obvious difference between the Ginnie Mae–guaranteed MBS and the Ginnie Mae–guaranteed HMBS is that the forward mortgages generate cash as the mortgages in the pool amortize while HECMs accrue interest until principal is due, which is when a maturity event occurs. Most HECMs take the form of floating-rate lines of credit. The line of credit is not revolving but is drawn down to its net principal limit over the person's tenure in the mortgaged property. In an HMBS securitization, the lender pools credit draws or annuity payments.

In Figure 11.3 there are three borrowers. Each has a different principal limit and each draws down the credit line at different times and the maturity event for each borrower is different. The first draw for each borrower can include all of the upfront fees that must be paid by the borrower; mortgage insurance premium (MIP), servicing fees, and origination and closing costs. The Ginnie Mae HMBS program requires that the lender either buy back or assign to FHA any HECM whose loan balance reaches 98 percent of the maximum claim amount (MCA). This requirement reduces the likelihood

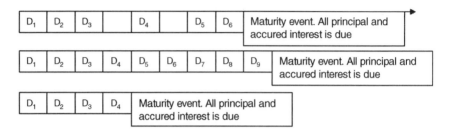

FIGURE 11.3 Hypothetical Variations of Cash Inflows and Outflows by Pooled HECM

that issuers will include poorly underwritten loans and it places an upper bound on the HECM obligations in a securitized pool. As the liability hits the 98 percent limit, it is taken out of the pool. When the mortgage is purchased out of the pool, the fund's principal and accrued interest are passed through to the investor. The lender has the option of putting HECMs to the FHA when the loan balance hits 98 percent of the MCA.

HECM SECURITIZATION

At first glance, one might think that there are similarities between the securitization of credit card receivables and HECMs because both obligations give the obligor the ability to draw credit periodically. It is possible that the structure that GNMA has put in place to securitize HECMs may evolve and become more similar to a credit card structure, but for now the two schemes are quite different.

In a typical credit card securitization it is the account activity of borrowers that is securitized. Investors are insulated from short-term variations in account balances by an interest in the securitized pool, called the *seller's interest*. The seller's interest absorbs fluctuations so that the investors can be offered medium-term stable bullet securities. If there is a long-term trend of increasing credit card account balances, the financial institution (the seller) can issue another series of notes from the same securitization vehicle if a master structure was used. An event that triggers an amortization of the outstanding securities, such as delinquency levels hitting a predetermined percent of the pool balance, would direct all cash flows from obligors to pay down the asset-backed securities.

In the case of the HMBS, the issuer securitizes participations in HECMs. GNMA defines the participation as the following: "A HECM participation is defined as the drawn amount of a HECM loan that a lender has securitized in a Ginnie Mae HMBS. Participations may be of any size and there will be no limit on the number of participations in a HECM loan. Each HECM participation will have a unique identification number tied back to the underlying HECM loan. Ginnie Mae's HMBS participation structure allows issuers to securitize the outstanding balance on a HECM, including mortgagor draws, accrued interest, servicing fees, and advances made to, or on behalf of the mortgagor. As the mortgagor's loan balance increases each month, all previously unsecuritized loan balances are eligible to be securitized as a new participation in a Ginnie Mae HMBS" (Mortgage-Backed Securities Program, Home Equity Conversion Mortgage (HECM) Reference Guide, Government National Mortgage Association, 2007).

In reference to Figure 11.3 and the definition of a *participation*, an HMBS can be composed of the Draws (D_i) across HECMS. The (D_i) can be from a single period or across periods. A single HECM can be refinanced with numerous participations, which may serve as collateral for either the same or different HMBSs. Our example distributes the participations across different HMBSs.

Borrowers can finance the closing costs and fees, which then become part of the securitized participation. The underlying credits in participation can be fixed rate or adjustable rate. Adjustable-rate credit can be indexed to either 1-month or 1-year LIBOR. GNMA requires that HECMs that are set to 1-year LIBOR have a limit on adjustments of 2 percent per year and 5 percent over the life of the loan. HECMs that are gauged to 1-month LIBOR must have a lifetime cap but are not required to have a yearly rate cap. Investors will view the cap as a potential hazard if market rates are expected to cause the HECM collateral to hit their caps. Pool data allows investors to estimate the probability that the caps will impact value and to what extent. HMBSs cannot be composed of both fixed-rate HECMs and adjustable-rate HECMs and adjustable HECMs in a pool must have the same index. Reset dates can differ. GNMA charges a servicing fee to the issuer.

The minimum pool size for an HMBS securitization is three participations from a single issuer that together must have a balance of at least $1,000,000. No more than 999 participations can be drawn from a single HECM. An HMBS is the first step to creating a liquid market. FNMA, Freddie Mac, and GNMA pass-through securities are the core of the secondary mortgage market serving as the collateral for REMICs, which enable the distillation and distribution of mortgage risk. As the supply of HECMs increases, the HMBS will be the core of the secondary market in reverse mortgages. The GNMA REMICs that securitize HMBS will broaden the market and give investors opportunities to take positions on HECMs that offer cash flow and risk profiles that are more consistent with their portfolios than would be a portfolio of the HMBSs. On the other side, the HMBS will lower the cost of liquidating home equity without having to give up the use of one's home. A financial innovation lowers the cost of capital for borrowers and expands the opportunities for investors. If HECMs can do this without requiring a positive subsidy from HUD, then they qualify as a financial innovation.

The HMBS pass-through accrual rate is the weighted average of the pool participation rates. The participation rate of each HECM in the pool is the accrual rate less the servicing fee. This servicing fee includes compensation for servicing as well as a guaranty fee that accrues payable to GNMA.

The rationale for the HMBS is succinctly stated by Ginnie Mae: "Securitization of HECM loans will result in a savings of 50 basis points or more for the borrower. On an average HECM loan of $118,000, this savings amounts to over $10,000 over a 10-year period, the average life of a HECM loan" (*Ginnie Mae Mortgage-Backed Securities Program Home Equity Conversion Mortgage (HECM) Reference Guide*, GNMA, May 2007).

The first HMBS was issued in 2006. In 2008, a second pool of HECMs was securitized. In 2009, there were 16 HMBSs issued by six different issuers for an amount of $853 million (Mortgage Bankers Association, "Secondary Market Update: MBA's Reverse Mortgage Lending Conference," September 11, 2009, Craig Corn, MetLife, Inc., John Kozak, Ginnie Mae, and Chris Witeck, Buckley Sandler, LLP). It is interesting to examine the pool information for a specific HMBS. For example, the HMBS prospectus supplement annex for GNMA Pool #892041 gives detailed financial and demographic information regarding the gender, geographic, and age of the borrowers whose participations have been securitized. This information must be the basis for making predictions about longevity, tenure, home price appreciation, and interest accrual rates. This HMBS was issued by World Alliance Financial Corporation on March 1, 2009. The pool consisted of 136 participations. The ratio of the pool balance to the principal limit on the issue date was .665.

In 2009, the first REMIC backed by HMBS LIBOR–indexed HECMs was issued. It was the Guaranteed HECM MBS REMIC Pass-Through Securities Ginnie Mae REMIC Trust 2009-H01. The trust financed $130,876,963 of HMBSs with three classes of securities. The FA class was an *accrual* pass-through class; the FI class was an accrual *interest-only* class. The third class was the residual.

In 2010, Guaranteed HECM MBS REMIC Pass-Through Securities and MX Securities Ginnie Mae REMIC Trust 2010-H01was issued. The principal amount of HMBSs financed by this trust was $142,845,088. The complexity in structuring of these REMICs lies in allocating distributions of uncertain future accrued interest and principal receipts that are tied to future interest rate paths and the timing of maturity events affecting the

HECMs that secure the HMBS. For example, in the 2009 REMIC, the FI class bears the burden of longevity risk and interest rate risk since the magnitude of cash flows investors receive depend on the interest path and the dates the HECMs are paid off. If tenure in the mortgage properties turns out to be shorter than expected, the FI class will receive less interest and this loss might be compounded by a decline in interest rates. The FA accrual class is more certain with respect to the timing of cash flows since it is structured to receive both principal and interest. Class FA is a more balanced security since the effects of shorter tenure are offset by the faster return of principal. The FI class is leveraged with respect to longevity/tenure risk.

Standardization within Ginnie Mae programs has enabled the market for Ginnie Mae MBSs to become one of the mainstays of the secondary mortgage market along with FNMA and Freddie Mac guaranteed pass-through securities. GNMA is a department within HUD. GNMA does not buy mortgages or MBSs; it *guarantees* MBSs. The majority of HECMs are structured as credit lines at floating rates. The GNMA HMBS is designed as a pass-through security but the quirk is that payments of interest and principal do not flow regularly. Interest accrues on outstanding principal and the repayment of principal occurs whether the borrower chooses to repay or when the home is sold. The borrower is not obligated to make any interest or principal payments until a maturity event takes place.

LONGEVITY RISK EMBEDDED IN HECM

The cash flow profile of an HECM is somewhat similar to that of life settlement contracts. A life settlement contract is created when an owner of a life insurance policy sells the policy to a third party. The buyer of the policy becomes the beneficiary of the death benefit but must also make the periodic premium payments. The value of the premium payments and the death benefits of life settlement contracts is predicted using mortality tables adjusted for health impairments. Once a sizable pool of life settlement contracts has been accumulated and priced according to the appropriate mortality table, the timing of the cash flows of both premiums and death benefits should fall within predictable bands.

In the case of HECMs it is necessary to predict how long the borrower will live in the property, the value of the property at the time when the person ceases to live in the property, and the rate at which interest will accrue on outstanding loan amounts. These factors must be modeled so that the Federal Housing Authority (FHA) guarantees that the lender will be made whole for any shortfalls between the HECM balance and the home value at the time the loan comes due. The FHA structures its protection by constraining the present value of HECM at origination to a fraction of the property value. The fraction is a function of the borrower's age (youngest of a couple), the rate at which interest is expected to compound on the outstanding loan balance, and the borrower's expected tenure in the property. Based on these factors a principal limit factor (PLF) is calculated. This PLF is then multiplied by an amount known as the *maximum claim amount (MCA)*, which is the lesser of the appraised value of the property or the FHA loan limit. As of now, the FHA loan limit is $625,000. Under provisions of the recent CR, the national FHA loan limit for HECM in 2010 remains at $625,500 (150 percent of the national conforming limit) (U.S. Department of Housing and Urban Development, Washington, D.C. 20410-8000, Assistant Secretary for Housing–Federal Housing Commissioner, www.hud.gov espanol.hud.gov, November 25, 2009, Mortgagee Letter 2009-50).

Table 11.1 is a sample PLF table published by the FHA. The factors increase as age of the borrower increases and decline as the rate of interest increases. For a 62-year-old borrower with an interest rate of 3 percent, the principal limit factor is .562. For a 75-year-old borrower the factor increases to .658. The tables are constructed up to age 99. When the accrual rate increases to 6 percent, the factor for a 62-year-old will decline to .507 and for a 75-year-old borrower the factor is .620. The decline in the factor when rates rise is necessary to limit the loan balance because more interest will accrue over the same timeframe. Without adjusting down the PV of the loan amount (principal limit), the chance that the loan balance will exceed the home value increases. This is known as *crossover risk*. When the age of the borrower increases this crossover risk declines because interest will accrue for a shorter time. This means that older people can borrow more via an HECM. A factor of .658 means that the gross amount of funds a borrower who owns a home valued at $500,000 could borrow by issuing an HECM would be $329,000. This amount would be reduced by origination fees, mortgage insurance, and servicing fees. Borrowers can finance the fees. It is important to understand that all of the choices a borrower has regarding the timing of how the lender distributes the funds must be ex-ante constrained to an equivalent present value. The tenure choice gives the borrower an annuity for as long as the mortgaged property is the borrower's primary residence. The term choice gives the borrower an equal monthly payment for a fixed number of periods. The line of credit can be drawn down to the principal limit amount, which increases at the rate of interest the borrower must pay on the loan balance, including previously accumulated interest. Of course the future is uncertain with regard to longevity and interest rates so that ex-post the present value of the choices will likely be very different from ex-ante expectations.

TABLE 11.1 FHA Principal Limit Factors by Age and Interest Rates

Age	Interest1	Factor1
62	3.00	.562
63	3.00	.569
64	3.00	.576
65	3.00	.584
66	3.00	.591
67	3.00	.598
68	3.00	.605
69	3.00	.612
70	3.00	.620
71	3.00	.628
72	3.00	.635
73	3.00	.643
74	3.00	.650
75	3.00	.658
62	6.00	.507
63	6.00	.515
64	6.00	.523
65	6.00	.531
66	6.00	.540
67	6.00	.549
68	6.00	.557
69	6.00	.566
70	6.00	.575
71	6.00	.584
72	6.00	.593
73	6.00	.602
74	6.00	.611
75	6.00	.620

The HUD web site provides a link to a calculator supplied by the National Reverse Mortgage Lenders Association (NRMLA), which enables borrowers to get an approximation of how much equity and at what cost the HECM can provide. The flowing calculations are based on a 75-year-old living in Nassau County, New York, in a home appraised at $500,000. The output is based on the current market rates and lender's margins appearing in lines one and two. The interest rate choices portrayed are: 1-month LIBOR, Fixed Rate and 1-Year LIBOR. We chose not to draw any funds in year zero for the two variable rates. When the fixed-rate choice is made, the borrower is obligated to receive all of the funds at origination.

Net principal available under each interest rate is different. Amounts available at origination, the initial principal limit, decline as interest rates increase. Under the 1-year LIBOR choice, the amount available from the credit line at future dates grows at a faster rate, albeit from a lower base than the 1-month LIBOR case. The interest rate cap on the 1-year LIBOR is 2 percent per year and 5 percent over the life of the loan. The rate on an HECM indexed to 1-month LIBOR is uncapped. This means that if sufficient funds are drawn early on, then the rate can potentially rise by enough to pull the loan balance above the value of the home. It is important to note that HECMs that serve as collateral for GNMA HMBS must have lifetime interest rate caps even if the rate is based on 1-month LIBOR.

THE CONSTRAINTS OF THE UNDERLYING ASSET

Because the HECM is nonrecourse, the borrower is not obligated to pay more than the value of the home but equity that was counted on to finance future consumption can become an asset of the lender. The 1-month LIBOR HECM will offer borrowers more funds but will expose more equity to risk. In 2008, 2.6 percent of HECMs were priced using a fixed interest rate and only .26 percent were priced using 1-year LIBOR. The remaining 97.14 percent of HECMs were priced on a 1-month LIBOR index.

Mortgage insurance premium (MIP) is added to the loan rate. The total loan rate compounded monthly yields the credit line growth rate. The loan principal limit is calculated based on the HECM expected rate. Loan principal limit is gross and from this amount servicing fees for the expected life of the loan are set aside to give the available principal limit. From the available principal limit origination fees, mortgage insurance fees and closing costs are netted out to arrive at the net principal limit. In the example we have used, we put the upfront cash payment at zero and did not make any initial draws under the credit line. This leaves the total net principal limit to grow at the initial credit line growth rate. (See Table 11.2.)

A report by the GAO explains very clearly how the maximum loan amount the FHA will insure under the HECM program is calculated (Report to Congressional Committees, U.S. Government Accountability Office (GAO), July 2009, "Reverse Mortgages: Policy Changes Have Had Mostly Positive Effects on Lenders and Borrowers, but These Changes and Market Developments Have Increased HUD's Risk," GAO-09-836).

Step 1: Calculate the maximum claim amount (MCA). This is the lesser of the FHA loan limit or the home value. In 2009, the FHA loan limit was increased to xx.

TABLE 11.2 National Reverse Mortgage Lenders Association (NRMLA) Calculations of Available Equity via HECM

You Could Get Interest adjusts >	HUD HECM 1-Month LIBOR Monthly	HUD HECM Fixed Rate –	HUD HECM 1-Year LIBOR Annual
Interest rate index	0.245%	—	0.876%
Plus lender's margin	3.000%	—	6.000%
Initial loan interest rate	3.245%	5.750%	6.876%
Plus mortgage insurance	0.50%	0.50%	0.50%
Initial total loan rate	3.745%	6.250%	7.376%
Initial credit line growth rate	3.810%	—	7.630%
Lifetime cap on loan rate	13.245%	5.750%	11.876%
HECM expected rate	6.720%	5.75%	9.720%
Monthly service fee	$ 30.00	$ 30.00	$ 30.00
Value of the home	$ 500,000	$500,000	$ 500,000
Home value limit	$ 625,500	$625,500	$ 625,500
Lesser of limit or home value	$ 500,000	$500,000	$ 500,000
Loan principal limit	$ 282,500	$319,500	$ 193,000
Less service fee set aside	$ 4,187	$ 4,571	$ 3,274
Available principal limit Less financed items	$ 278,313	$314,929	$ 189,727
Loan origination fee	$ 6,000	$ 6,000	$ 6,000
Mortgage insurance	$ 10,000	$ 10,000	$ 10,000
Other closing costs	$ 8,559	$ 8,559	$ 8,559
Net principal limit	$ 253,755	$290,370	$ 165,168
Less lump-sum cash	$ 0	$290,370	$ 0
Less selected credit line	$ 0	$ 0	$ 0
Left for monthly advance	$ 253,755	$ 0	$ 165,168
Monthly advance	$ 1,818	$ 0	$ 1,514
No more lien payments	+0.00	+0.00	+0.00
Increase in monthly cash	$1,818.32	$ 0.00	$1,513.68
Monthly term	Tenure	Tenure	Tenure
Total fees and costs	$ 24,559	$ 24,559	$ 24,559

Source: National Reverse Mortgage Lenders Association, http://rmc.ibisreverse.com/default_nrmla.aspx.

Step 2: Calculate the principal limit factor. The principal limit factor accounts for loan termination rates. Loan termination rates are a function of mortality rates and move-out rates. In addition, the principal limit factor must incorporate the projected value of the house and loan balance at the loan termination date. The principal limit is based on the expected home appreciation rate, interest rates on the loan, and the mortgagor's expected life span.

Step 3: The MCA is multiplied by the PLF. This yields the gross loan amount.

Step 4: Up front and periodic fees are netted out of this amount to give the loan funds available. The upfront fees include mortgage insurance premiums (MIPs) and the origination fee. The periodic costs are for servicing. The present value of the periodic costs out to 100 years of age is netted out of the loan amount.

Loan funds available may be drawn in a number of ways. Each choice should have the same expected value.

The constraint that the loan choices must not violate is that the present value of the difference between the home value and the expected debt at the time of a maturity event when discounted at the required rate of return is greater than or equal to zero. Higher rates of interest accrual will lead to higher loan balances at the time of a maturity event. This means that the difference between home value and loan balance (HV—LB) will be smaller at the maturity event date. To preserve the yield to the lender, the principal lent is reduced at origination. If at the time of the maturity event the HV is less than the LB, then the FHA would make the lender whole. The FHA guarantee is funded by the mortgage insurance premium (MIP) paid by the borrower. The MIP is 2 percent of the lesser of the appraised value of the home or the FHA HECM limit plus an additional .5 percent per month of the outstanding mortgage balance. The FHA standard HECM loan limits are now $625,000. Since the FHA is on the hook for any shortfalls between the HV and LB, loan amounts are governed by the FHA. The loan limit is used to constrain the present value of the loan amount. In other words, a borrower will receive only amounts that in future value terms are not expected to exceed the $625,000 limit. The terminology is a bit confusing since *loan limit* implies that this is the amount one can borrow.

A longer expected time to a maturity for a given fixed rate of interest or assumed interest rate path in the case of adjustable-rate HECMs diminishes the difference between HV and LB. Since younger borrowers are expected to live longer and remain longer in their current residence the HECM loan limits decline for younger borrowers in order to keep the difference between HV and LB wide enough to offer lenders the required expected rate of return.

These are complicated personal finance decisions. The FHA has recognized this complexity by requiring that all prospective HECM mortgagors receive financial counseling. The decision to opt for the credit line (the most popular choice) for the fixed term versus the cash flows over one's tenure in the property is an expression about current income constraints, expected longevity, and expected interest rates. If the PV of all loan options is the same as it should be if the HECM choices are designed fairly, then the choice is one of matching consumption needs with income. If payments are higher than what one needs to satisfy consumption, then the cost of carrying the unused funds is borne by the borrower. Untapped balances of the HECM credit line grow at the rate of interest charged to draws. This results in a growing balance over time.

The basics of HECMs are as follows:

- The HECM may be originated only by FHA-approved lenders.
- The HECM can be issued only by people who are age 62 and older to mortgage.
- The HECM can be used only to mortgage a primary residence.
- The HECM must constitute a first-priority lien on the mortgaged property.
- Once the HECM is issued, the mortgagor (borrower) is not obligated to repay principal or pay interest until a maturity event has occurred.

The most significant maturity event is that the borrower moves from the property. This can occur because the mortgagor passes away or chooses to move away. Other maturity events can be triggered by the mortgagor's failure to pay taxes or to keep the property properly insured, or if mortgagor allows the property to fall into disrepair.

Once a maturity event occurs, the borrower must repay the outstanding principal and accrued interest. Included in the principal amount of the loan upon which interest accrues are fees that are charged at origination and periodically over the term of the mortgage. These fees cover mortgage insurance premium, servicing, and closing costs.

The securitization of reverse mortgages is problematical because the nature of the cash flows generated by the asset is comparable to risky zero-coupon bonds with uncertain maturities. This means that the owner of the asset does not know what will be the value of the mortgaged asset at the unknown maturity date. Under the terms of the FHA HECM, the borrower is not required to repay loan principal or interest on the loan until the date the loan is due.

The PLF is calculated to build a layer of protection into the HECM. It is done by discounting the maximum claim amount down to a level that can support longevity risk, home price risk, and interest rate risk. Rising interest rates combined with higher-than-expected tenure in the property increase the likelihood that the FHA will experience losses from the guarantees of HECMs on its books. It is interesting to note that the ratio of IPL to MCA rose during the housing boom, indicating the FHA was taking on increased risk. The ratio turned before the bubble burst in 2005, indicating that the FHA already sensed the momentum in home prices would not continue. It is not clear to us why the ratio of IPL to MCA began rising again in 2006. It was already clear that housing prices were falling at a fast pace. (See Figure 11.4.)

The FHA's protection against losses on its HECM-guaranteed portfolio is equity in the home that cannot be reverse mortgaged. Equity above the principal limit amount cannot be reverse mortgaged. This layer of equity protects the FHA, which insures HECMs. To fund potential losses on its HECM obligations, the FHA collects an initial insurance fee and a monthly insurance fee. When the loan balance reaches 98 percent of the MCA, lenders can assign the HECM to the FHA. When HECMs are securitized through the Ginnie Mae HMBS program, they are obligated to buy back from the securitized pool HECMs that have loan balances greater than or equal to 98 percent of the MCA. The lender having bought the HECM out

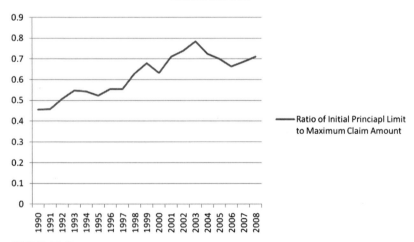

FIGURE 11.4   Ratio of Initial Principal Limit to Maximum Claim Amount

of the pool can then put it to the FHA. GNMA charges an additional guarantee fee. The FHA guarantee and the GNMA guarantees are distinct. GNMA guarantees the performance of HMBSs. The FHA guarantee makes the lender whole in the case that the home value cannot cover the loan amount, and accrued interest makes the borrower whole if the lender cannot fulfill its obligations under the HECM contract.

CONCLUDING REMARKS

Liquidity is being enhanced by Ginnie Mae development of a pass-through security backed by the HECM, the Ginnie Mae Guaranteed Home Equity Conversion Mortgage-Backed Security, and the Ginnie Mae Guaranteed HECM MBS REMIC Pass-Through Security. The market for Ginne Mae pass-through securities backed by conventional mortgages is well established and has been a firm foundation for the secondary market in mortgages. GNMA is a department within the U.S. federal agency Housing and Urban Development. The GNMA guarantee is backed by the full faith and credit of the United States. This places GNMA-guaranteed securities at par with U.S. Treasuries with regard to credit risk. The nature of HECMs makes them a difficult instrument to manage unless one has a large portfolio. This is due to the fact that the maturity date of the HECM is uncertain and payment of interest and principal is not due until a maturity event occurs.

Longevity and tenure risk are the primary uncertainties associated with HECMs. Longevity and tenure risks affect the yield investors receive on HECMs and assets backed by HECMs because the accrued interest and timing of the payoff are directly tied to how long the property is occupied by the mortgagors. Credit risk is also a function of longevity and tenure in the property because the longer the property remains mortgaged the more likely it is that the value of the loan will exceed the value of the property.

In a CRS report ("Reverse Mortgages: Background and Issues," updated April 8, 2008, Bruce E. Foote, Analyst in Housing, Domestic Social Policy Division, Congressional Research Service), it is noted that 12.5 million senior citizens own their homes free and clear. That is, their homes are not mortgaged. The median home value of these homes is stated at $127,959. A quick back-of-the-envelope calculation based on this median value places the potential for the reverse mortgage market at over $1 trillion. This number merely refers to a point in time. Each year, the number of people who turn 62 (the minimum age to qualify for an HECM) increases. With the increasing longevity, frequency of financial shocks, and increasing uncertainty of expenses, a household's home equity becomes an important source of income. The reverse mortgage enables people to remain in their homes while trading illiquid equity for cash. The HECM offers seniors a reliable source of cash that can be tapped when needed. In fact, the longer that a household waits to tap into the home equity via an HECM, the more equity they can take out. The HECM becomes a call option on home equity. This is important since this option to call out home equity via an HECM is a prudent way of supplementing long-term heath care or heath insurance while retaining the benefits of homeownership. Option valuation may be a way of analyzing the HECM and securities derived from the HECM cash flows. GNMA's efforts to develop a secondary market in HECMS will increase the flow of capital into the market. HECMs should become a useful tool in financial planning as intergenerational wealth transfers from current to future generations decline due to increased longevity.

SUMMARY

In this chapter we have discussed how the efforts of HUD and the Government National Mortgage Association have resulted in a robust primary market for reverse mortgages and a burgeoning secondary market in this important asset class. In coming years, senior citizens will face tightening financial constraints. The home equity conversion mortgage is a financial innovation that will loosen these constraints. The HMBS and the HMBS REMIC are innovations that offer investors a reliable asset class that provides exposure to various levels of longevity risk and tenure risk at market-compensating yields. Whereas financial innovation may have a negative stigma in the press due to the collapse of the private-label mortgage-backed security market, financial innovation will play a very important role going forward as households, enterprises, and sovereigns are challenged to manage more inter-temporal cash flows in an increasingly uncertain world. Financial engineering is the key to creating a liquid security from illiquid reverse mortgages that would be a drain on a financial institution's capital if the reverse mortgage had to remain on balance sheet.

BHUYAN'S FINAL POINTS

- As traditional markets become overcrowded and increasingly more volatile, investors will need to seek out opportunities in more esoteric investments such as reverse mortgages.

- The ability to address liquidity issues with reverse mortgages via structured products will drive investor appetite for the RM asset class and other life-linked assets such as life settlements.
- Securitization of reverse mortgages hinges on accurately forecasting the mortality curve associated with the underlying pool of loans.

Housing Wealth Among the Elderly

Olivia S. Mitchell
Insurance & Risk Management,
The Wharton School, University of Pennsylvania

John Piggott
School of Economics, University of New South Wales

A necessary precondition for the use of reverse mortgages (RMs) is the existence of private housing equity.[1] In developed countries, enormous wealth is held in residential property. Viewed from the perspective of strategic asset allocation, an owner-occupied dwelling is illiquid and undiversified. Indeed, elderly people on average possess greater housing wealth than the population average, but they can also have incomes that are much lower than those received by younger groups.

WEALTH IN HOUSING

We next turn to an examination of the characteristics of housing wealth and ownership among the elderly in three countries: the United States, Japan, and Australia. It should not be surprising to find that, in all three countries, home equity represents the largest component of household assets. In Japan, for instance, 51 percent of total assets were nonfinancial in 1996, and of these, home equity was by far the largest component (Ellis and Andrews). In Australia, housing assets amounted to 50 percent of all household assets according to a government 1996 survey.[2] In the United States, housing equity comprised 44 percent of all household wealth, much higher than the second largest component, interest-bearing securities, according to a Census Bureau survey in 1995.[3]

We caution that these figures are not precisely comparable, since each deals with slightly different accounting measures. Yet the implication is clear: Residents in each country hold a substantial amount of wealth in residential property. Moreover, these heavy weightings in property might indicate that households seeking to increase current consumption by reducing assets would, in line with modern portfolio theory, look to home equity first.

In all three countries, the amount of housing equity generally increases with age. Japan exhibits this trend in the most consistent fashion. Figure A.1 reports average net and gross dwelling values for Japanese households of varying ages in 1999. The positive association of home equity with age is clear: The most senior households in Japan have the greatest housing equity, with at least 35 million yen. Australia, too, offers a similar picture, but unlike Japan, the oldest cohort does not have the greatest amount of housing equity. Among people aged 65+, mean home equity was $A 155,000 in 1995–1996, 8 percent higher than the average for all owner-occupiers.[4] Figure A.2 illustrates the U.S. data, which demonstrates the same general

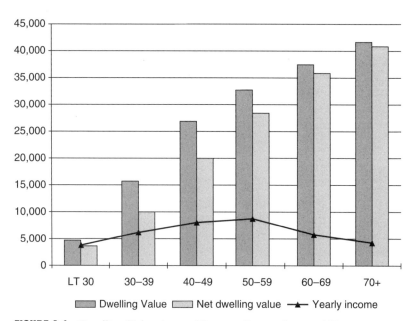

FIGURE A.1 Dwelling Value Age and Income: Japan, thousand Yen
Source: NSFIES (1999, Table 21), www.stat.go.jp/data/zensho/1999/z.

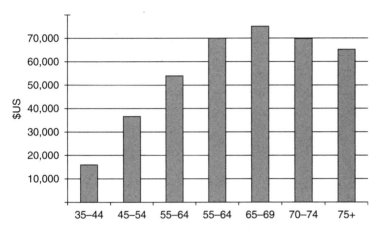

FIGURE A.2 Median Home Equity by Age: United States
Source: U.S. Census Bureau (1995), *Asset Ownership of Households.*

pattern as Australia: Housing equity rises for younger people, but then it begins to decline after age 64. Yet the elderly still have substantial median housing equity, in 1995 being worth at least one-third more than the median housing equity ($US 50,000).[5] These figures demonstrate that, on average, elderly people hold more housing equity than do their younger contemporaries. Moreover, the value of this equity is significant, and it could easily be used to supplement retirement income.

In the case of Japan, at least, Figure A.1 shows that income and assets are not positively correlated; indeed, average income falls with age after ages 50–59. This might indicate that elderly Japanese households would be desirous of some mechanism that would enable them to maintain their income at a reasonably sustained level. This substantial home equity could be the means by which they facilitate this end.

Figure A.3 compares the housing wealth of all households and of the elderly in thousands of $US across the three countries. The data has been adjusted to reflect year-2000 prices and has been converted using *purchasing power parity* exchange rates. The gross and net values for the elderly in each country do not vary much, indicating that these households have relatively little housing debt. The salient feature of this graph is the huge discrepancy between the high values of Japanese properties on the one hand, and the lower Australian and U.S. properties on the other. Evidently, elderly Japanese have housing equity almost 50 percent greater than their foreign counterparts.

One reason this is so is that living patterns in Japan differ from those in western countries, there being a strong tendency for many elderly in Japan

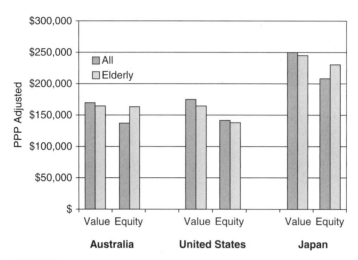

FIGURE A.3 Average Home Values and Equity
Sources: ABS (1999), *Australian Housing Survey*; RAND Corporation (1998), *Health and Retirement Survey*, Wave 5; Economagic (online resource); World Bank (2002), *World Development Indicators*, Table 5.6.

to live with their children. Consequently, this pattern might be biased toward rich elderly Japanese households.[6] As Figure A.3 indicates, however, the value of houses held by other age groups in Japan, though less than that of the elderly, is also vastly higher than Australian and U.S. values for elderly people. Further, Japanese living arrangements are rapidly approaching those in western countries. In 1998, some 45 percent of elderly Japanese lived apart from their children, compared to only 27 percent in 1980 (Ishikawa and Yajima, 2001).

All these facts augur well for RMs in Japan, since they demonstrate that elderly households have substantial housing equity, as a proportion of total assets, absolutely, and in comparison to other age groups. Moreover, in light of these statistics, Japan seems to offer a potentially even more favorable environment for such products than do Australia and the United States.

OWNER-OCCUPANCY RATES

A second essential precondition of a successful RMs market is that people must own their homes. Renters lack home equity to convert to current consumption, and thus they cannot avail themselves of the benefits of RMs. The data show, however, that aggregate owner-occupancy rates are quite high in all three countries of special interest here. Figure A.4 compares the

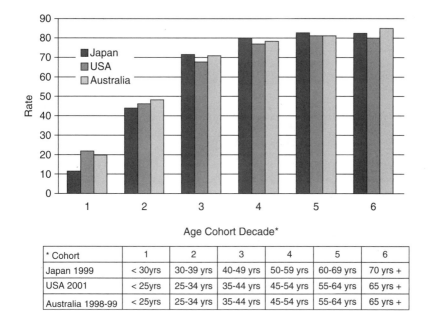

* Cohort	1	2	3	4	5	6
Japan 1999	< 30yrs	30-39 yrs	40-49 yrs	50-59 yrs	60-69 yrs	70 yrs +
USA 2001	< 25yrs	25-34 yrs	35-44 yrs	45-54 yrs	55-64 yrs	65 yrs +
Australia 1998-99	< 25yrs	25-34 yrs	35-44 yrs	45-54 yrs	55-64 yrs	65 yrs +

FIGURE A.4 Owner-Occupier Rates by Age: Japan, United States, Australia
Sources: U.S. Census Bureau, *Housing Vacancy Survey* (Q2, 2002); Statistics Bureau
& Statistics Center, *Housing of Japan*; Management & Coordination Agency (May
2000), *Household Expenditure Survey Australia*.

owner-occupancy rates for the three countries by age group, and it confirms
that the clear trend is for owner-occupancy rates, like home equity, to increase with age. Indeed, rates hover around 80 percent for owner-occupiers
aged 65+, implying that a very high proportion of the elderly occupies and
owns the same home. Such high rates, combined with the high housing
equity examined above, underscore the substantial potential for RMs in
Japan.

HOW RISKY IS HOUSING WEALTH?

The tendency for households to retain much of their wealth in the form of
housing equity is discussed above, and it has been well documented in the
western nations.[7] This pattern no doubt flows from both social tradition
and tax policy favoring housing, yet it may not be such a good idea from an
economic perspective, given the price volatility of real estate.[8] Figures A.5
and A.6 show the price movements of real estate in five major international
cities and four major countries, respectively.

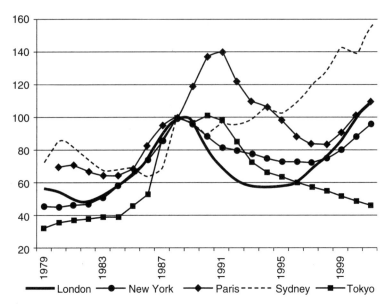

FIGURE A.5   Cross-City Comparison of Real House Prices
Source: Authors' computations using data provided by *The Economist*.

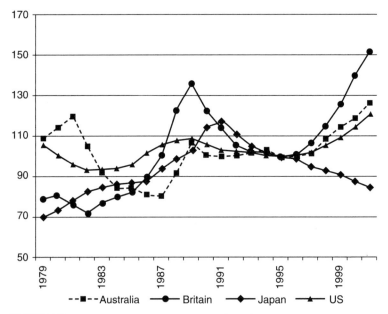

FIGURE A.6   Cross-Country Comparison of Real House Prices
Source: Authors' computations using data provided by *The Economist*.

The graphs clearly indicate that real estate can be quite volatile over the medium and long term. Price increases and decreases of over 40 percent within five years are not rare; Tokyo prices, in particular, exhibit erratic price behavior. Consequently, there is concern that elderly households could be concentrating too much of their wealth in a home, subjecting themselves to a single volatile investment in real estate.

Unfortunately, there is relatively little economic research that evaluates housing price volatility into models of life-cycle asset allocation, despite the obvious importance of owner-occupier housing in the portfolios of most retirees. For instance, Poterba (2001) points out that in the United States, real property accounted for about one-third of total financial assets in 2000, or about US$13 trillion. Flavin and Yamashita (2002) also confirm that few studies of household asset choice incorporate housing as an asset. They then propose that substantial transactions costs for housing purchase and sale mean that portfolio adjustment occurs on margins other than housing. Their analysis finds that the return to housing in the United States is uncorrelated with stocks, Treasury bills, and bonds. Because young households are often highly leveraged with a housing mortgage, one response is to hold bonds when young, and increase the weighting on stocks when households grow older. This view is supported by Cocco (2000), who also argues that the life-cycle pattern of homeownership can explain why the proportion of wealth held in stocks tends to increase with age.

Even if households wished to reduce some of their exposure to real estate, high transaction costs and a lack of appropriate financial products might prevent them from doing so. As Caplin (1999) argues, a method to unlock home equity could therefore be a very valuable risk management tool and also a mechanism to meet consumption needs for elderly households.

DO THE ELDERLY DECUMULATE THEIR HOUSING WEALTH?

An RM-type product will succeed only if homeowners are prepared to draw down their housing wealth in retirement. There is substantial debate about whether and to what extent this occurs, and the empirical evidence is mixed. U.S. research by Venti and Wise (2001) shows that a decline in housing equity only takes place at the age of 75 and then at a rate of 1.76 percent per annum. Moreover, if households receiving adverse financial shocks are excluded, the decline is a mere 0.11 percent per annum. The authors conclude that the American elderly do not liquidate their homes to support their general consumption needs as they age. Sheiner and Weil (1993),

TABLE A.1 Housing Status Change at Death of Spouse

Years Since Death of Spouse	Women Fraction Owning	Average Dwelling Value (USD)	Men Fraction Owning	Average Dwelling Value (USD)
−4	0.78	37,775	0.85	40,728
−3	0.77	38,061	0.85	39,668
−2	0.79	37,531	0.84	42,827
−1	0.76	40,281	0.80	40,592
0	0.76	37,952	0.79	41,763
1	0.72	36,511	0.77	43,257
2	0.71	34,549	0.71	38,407
3	0.68	34,098	0.76	39,184
4.	0.64	32.733	0.75	

Source: Sheiner and Weil (1993).

however, come to a different conclusion, finding instead a decline in home equity at older ages, mainly associated with shocks to family status and health, or the death of a spouse. Table A.1 shows the decline in both owner-occupancy rates and dwelling values in the years leading up to, and after, the death of a spouse.

Such information demonstrates that housing equity at older ages does decline. Table A.2 further illustrates this phenomenon by examining cohorts of elderly at different ages and at five-year intervals. Each cohort exhibits a decline in its ownership rate as it ages; again, however, notable declines mainly take place at considerably advanced ages, especially after age 80. Thus reductions in home equity in America are primarily incited by adverse unforeseen shocks, and even then these are most seen among the "old" elderly.

TABLE A.2 Change in Ownership Status among the Elderly

Age in 1988	Women Owner-Occupier Rate in 1983	Change in Ownership (1983–1988)	Men Owner-Occupier Rate in 1983	Change in Ownership (1983–1988)
60–64	0.80	−0.02	0.82	−0.01
65–69	0.78	−0.01	0.82	0.00
70–74	0.74	−0.05	0.81	0.00
75–79	0.67	−0.02	0.79	−0.01
80–84	0.63	−0.07	0.79	−0.08
85–89	0.53	−0.05	0.73	−0.09

Source: Sheiner and Weil (1993).

Such findings must be interpreted with some caution, especially if seen as a possible indicator of the likely behavior of future cohorts. First, depreciation of the housing stock could be occurring, unrevealed by the data. Second, low drawdown may be associated with a lack of means of secure drawdown— home equity loans leave the owner vulnerable to foreclosure. Third, RM contracts are now proliferating in the United States. Hence, the currently working generation, in all three exemplar countries, has fewer children and so may reduce the target value of intended bequests to reflect this.

The pattern of housing value drawdown by age in Japan is investigated by Ishikawa and Yajima (2001). These authors note that the Japanese elderly do exhibit negative saving after the age of 65, but it appears to happen via the liquidation of financial assets, not housing assets. This finding can be seen as consistent with the analysis of Flavin and Yamashita (2002), cited earlier. The authors posit that elderly Japanese households on average leave an estate equivalent to 25.8 years of consumption. The untouched value of the home equity accounts for 20.5 years, and the remainder is accounted for by unused financial assets (bank deposits, securities, etc.). By contrast, they estimate that the elderly in the United States leave behind only 5 years of consumption.

Of course, this huge disparity might not reflect different intentions or preferences, but rather a poorly performing Japanese housing market and financial sector that do not provide secure means of housing wealth drawdown. This point is expanded upon later in this study, but for now, we note the low level of market activity in the Japanese housing market. Table A.3 shows that this market is only one-tenth as active as the American market, and it focuses on the construction of new dwellings rather than the purchase of existing ones. Furthermore, the Japanese elderly move only one-quarter as frequently as their American counterparts, which could be the result of the emaciated housing market.

Current related research suggests that in Australia and Japan, at least, households have mostly paid off their mortgages at retirement. This

TABLE A.3 Moving Rates of Owner Households Age 65 and Over

	Japan (1998)%	United States (1997)%
(1997)% Owner households who moved	0.72	2.9
—to another owner-occupied home	0.45	1.67
—to a rented home	0.26	1.22
Renter households who moved	3.75	8.16

Source: Ishikawa and Yajima (2001).

behavior is consistent with a reluctance to draw down housing wealth in retirement. In the United States, however, retirees have more housing debt. A possible explanation for this lies in tax provisions. Interest on housing debt in the United States is tax-deductible, whereas this is not the case in Australia or Japan. In turn, this points to the importance of clear regulations and rules concerning concomitant liability with RMs, if such an initiative is to succeed. It would be of interest to further investigate whether, and to what extent, Japanese households draw down their housing wealth. Nishimura et al. (1999) argue that housing, and particularly land, operates as a tax shelter under Japan's tax structure (see also Seko, 1994a, b).

Various attempts have been made to explain why housing wealth is not drawn down sooner and more fully by the elderly. Two frequently proffered reasons are the desire to leave bequests, and precautionary saving. A bequest motive presumes that the elderly wish to leave some or all of their estate as a gift for their heirs. Again, there is conflicting evidence surrounding this issue. Hurd (2001) constructs a model for bequests and tests it using U.S. data; he finds that when one's mortality risk becomes sufficiently high, housing decumulation does indeed commence. Furthermore, he reports that the extent of decumulation is invariant across households with different numbers of children. Similar results have been reproduced by Haider et al. (2001), who find that in the 1970s and 1980s, households with and without children dissaved at the same rate. Moreover, some experts have argued that the Japanese do not exhibit strong bequest motives (Horioka, 2002; Ishikawa and Yajima, 2001). Further, little hard evidence supports the importance of bequest motives for the average worker or retiree. Of the people who applied for an RM in the United States, over 75 percent reported having no children (Caplin, 2002). At least in relation to RMs, then, it seems that people ostensibly less inclined to leave a bequest have been more frequent customers. The low Japanese fertility rate thus suggests that the development of a viable RM market in Japan may be more rather than less feasible.

Precautionary saving is another reason the elderly might wish to retain equity in their home. Older people may keep substantial equity in case unplanned expenditures arise, such as those associated with severe health problems. As yet, very little is known about how these events actually affect dissaving patterns (Haider et al., 2001). In any event, it seems unlikely that households would want to retain the entire value of their property for precautionary savings, especially as people knowingly come closer to their life expectancy.

It may also be true that these reasons affect consumption only at the margin. Thus, elderly people might want to use their housing equity more frequently, but their desire to remain in their homes might be a strongly dominant consideration, barring a health shock or marital status change. Indeed, Venti and Wise (2000) reported that 95 percent of Americans aged 75+ expressed a desire to remain in their current home for as long as possible. Transaction costs aside, such sentiments are inimical to the suggestion that a household simply move to a smaller residence in order to liquidate some of its housing equity. Given a pent-up desire to reduce home equity but remain in the family home, the utility of an RM becomes apparent.

We have seen that households generally do not decumulate their housing equity with age to the extent consistent with the simple life-cycle hypothesis. The desires to leave a bequest and for precautionary savings are logical explanations for this contradiction, but it seems unlikely that they can fully explain the enormous amount of housing equity that elderly households leave upon their death. In theory at least, the RM seems to be an excellent financial instrument for that proportion of elderly households who both wish to use some of their home equity to better enjoy their life and also wish to remain in the home. Finally, it is worth remembering that all these empirical results and research are endogenous to the currently prevailing pension systems. Were state-sponsored pensions to become substantially less generous, retirees might boost their reliance on home equity to finance old-age consumption.

NOTES

1. This refers to the population aged 65+ as a proportion of the working-age population.
2. See the *Year Book Australia* 2002 (ABS, 2002).
3. R. Disney and P. Johnson, *Pension Systems and Retirement Incomes Across OECD Countries* (Edward Elgar, 2001), 16.
4. See *The Economist*, May 28, 2002.
5. L. Ellis and D. Andrews, "City Sizes, Housing Costs, and Wealth," research discussion paper, Reserve Bank of Australia, October 2001.
6. When lending institutions hold assets that are perceived as relatively risky, such as mortgages, regulatory agencies will insist that the institutions increase their proportion of capital to facilitate greater confidence in repayment. Thus lenders like to sell some proportion of their mortgages to avoid the associated capital charges. Indeed, the new Basel Capital Adequacy provisions of 1999 specifically emphasize the importance of risk weighting in relation to assets. The relative riskiness of assets in institutions' portfolios is becoming a more important determinant of their capital requirements. This issue is therefore very relevant for RMs.

7. E. J. Szymanoski and T. R. DiVenti, "Demand and Supply Issues in RM Lending: The U.S. Experience and Its Implications for Eastern Europe and Russia," paper presented at the *International AREAUEA Conference*, Cancun, Mexico, May 2001.

8. R. J. Shiller and A. N. Weiss, "Home Equity Insurance," working paper DP 1074, Cowles Foundation, July 1994.

Reverse Mortgage Analytics

Olivia S. Mitchell
Insurance & Risk Management,
The Wharton School, University of Pennsylvania

John Piggott
School of Economics, University of New South Wales

At a general level, all reverse mortgage offerings that are self-financing must be priced so that the lending institution can expect to make back the money loaned plus interest over the term of the contract, after pooling risks across the set of loans sold. Here we provide an analysis of the lump-sum and annuity options for the reverse annuity product.

A simplified model of the loan amount can be specified by supposing a single borrower took out a loan in the form of a lump sum (LS) using his future home value as collateral. Then in a competitive market, the actuarially fair amount he could borrow would be set so the loan balance would equal in present value the anticipated value of the house at the time of sale. This may be defined as follows:

$$LS = \sum_{t=1}^{maxAge - x + 1} HEQ^* \frac{1 + r + g}{1 + r + m}^t {}^* {}_t p_x \qquad (B.1)$$

where r = expected future riskless rate of return, g = additional risk premium expected on housing investment above the riskless rate, m = additional risk premium expected on mortgage loans above the riskless rate, HEQ = home equity amount at the time the loan is taken out, ${}_t p$ = probability of survival t periods from age x, $maxAge$ = oldest possible survival age from life table (e.g., 110).

The lump sum *(LS)* simply grows at the mortgage rate *(r + m)*, and the total amount repayable *(Q)* after t periods is

$$Q = LS(1 + r + m)^t \tag{B.2}$$

The mathematics for a life annuity are more complicated. Again, the lender determines the actuarially fair maximum present value of an annuity *(LS)* that a borrower can purchase. The borrower then receives a fixed nominal payment per period until death. The nominal payment *(PMT)* is calculated thus:

$$PMT = LS \sum_{t=1}^{\omega} {}_t p_x \tag{B.3}$$

where r is the risk-free rate of interest, t is the number of payment periods until death, and ${}_t p_x$ is the annuitant's probability of survival t periods from age x. These equations form the basic structure of the RM products.

DETERMINING THE PAYOUT VALUES: PRACTICAL CONSIDERATIONS

In a practical setting, an RM lender would specify each of the model parameters, including the initial home value, the pattern of expected future riskless returns, expected future risk premia on the appreciation of the house and on mortgage loans, and the future mortality table that would apply to the borrower as well as the maximum possible age of survival.

This simple model could also be made more realistic in a practical setting, in several ways. First, the initial home value must be specified net of any remaining mortgage, if there is one. Second, the lender often demands that the home be brought into good repair at the outset, to protect the value of the lender's investment. In practice, needed repairs not only may be included in the value of the loan, but they also might be stipulated on an ongoing basis. Third, lenders must develop a forecast of future returns in developing the loan amount that can be provided, most importantly, for the riskless rate and the future mortgage rate. Since these are unknown, some sensitivity analysis is usually required.

Fourth, the lender must devise a forecast of each home's likely future appreciation, and here there is a distinct possibility of adverse selection and/or moral hazard. For instance, a homeowner who believed that his or her own home was deteriorating in value would be more likely to seek an

RM than average; furthermore, once an RM was obtained, the homeowner might be less likely to keep up the property.[1] Fifth, the lender must model not only the probability of home sale due to the borrower's death, but also the chance that the homeowner will terminate his residency due to other reasons, including the need to move into a nursing home and/or to move in with children. Data on actual termination rates are virtually impossible to obtain (Rodda et al., 2000), though early evidence in the United States indicates that younger homeowners are terminating their HECM loans more quickly than anticipated by the government insurers (Szymanoski and DiVenti, 2001).

A sixth consideration is that a lender must identify and/or develop the mortality table(s) appropriate to RM users. The illustration above specifies the survival pattern of a single individual, whereas in practice many elderly seeking RMs might be married couples. In that instance, using a joint-and-survivor table would likely be more appropriate than a single-female table. In addition, one must determine whether to use population or annuitant mortality tables, since the former expresses the entire nation's mortality experience, whereas the latter tends to have lower-than-average mortality patterns due to the fact that annuitants tend to be self-selected to live longer than average (McCarthy and Mitchell, 2002). A lender who uses a population table would then potentially be exposed to the possibility that those people who seek to borrow against their equity might actually have lighter-than-average mortality experience, akin to the degree of adverse selection found among annuity buyers. Whether this is appropriate is not yet known given relatively little experience with RMs, though RM buyers may be in worse health and require the housing loan to pay medical bills (in which case they would likely die earlier).[2] It is also unlikely that a lender would use a period life table, instead of a cohort table, since the former assumes fixed mortality rates over time whereas a cohort table builds in anticipated improvements in life expectancy. The latter is a more conservative stance, which would lead to a reduction in the amount that could be loaned on the house.

COMPUTING PAYOUT VALUES: AN EXAMPLE

To compute either the appropriate annuity payments or the lump sum amount that can be borrowed, a lender must develop assumptions regarding the evolution of interest rates, future home values, and mortality tables, as well as termination probabilities. Compared to the lump-sum approach mentioned earlier, both the line-of-credit and the annuity payout approach would postpone the time path of funds borrowed. In this event, the lender

TABLE B.1 Reverse Mortgage Lump-Sum or Monthly Payment (for Tenure in Home), by Age and Home Value: U.S. HECM and HomeKeeper Loans

	HECM	HomeKeeper	HECM	HomeKeeper
$100,000				
65	52,774	14,128	303	111
70	57,224	26,660	345	193
75	62,064	34,764	402	301
80	67,125	43,262	482	385
85	72,250	52,481	610	511
90	77,296	58,397	858	586
$300,000				
65	155,617	51,238	893	402
70	167,438	89,478	1010	647
75	180,176	112,428	1166	973
80	193,309	137,728	1389	1226
85	206,332	164,803	1743	1605
90	218,749	182,373	2427	1829

Source: www.rmaarp.com, viewed January 15, 2003 for zip 19004. Interest rate and closing costs assumed by calculator, based on 1-year Treasury bill returns for the week of January 13, 2003, plus servicing costs.

might either charge a lower mortgage rate for the delayed payout arrangement, or permit the borrower to obtain a larger fraction of his or her initial home equity, than under the lump-sum approach.

The data in Table B.1 illustrates a range of results for the U.S. context. The results are computed using a web site calculator provided by the AARP, a prominent and nationally known senior citizen organization. The data assumes the 1-year Treasury bill rates in effect at the time of computation and national average closing costs for RMs. Two sets of results are provided: those that would be available under the HECM program that are insured by the Federal Housing Administration, and those available via a proprietary RM program developed by Fannie Mae, known as the *Home-Keeper* mortgage.[3]

The data indicates that a 75-year-old with $100,000 in net home equity could obtain a federally insured HECM lump-sum home equity loan of about $62,000, versus a HomeKeeper loan of about 44 percent less or $34,800. Alternatively, the borrower could take the loan as a monthly payment as long as he remained in his home. For the 75-year-old with $100,000 in net equity, this would amount to around $402 per month, or $4,800 per year, in the HomeKeeper case; this annuity is 25 percent above the annual $3,600 generated by the HECM product. It is interesting that tripling the available home equity to $300,000 raises the lump sum obtainable by three times in the HECM case, but more than triples the lump sum payable by the HomeKeeper product. In the annuity flows, the HECM annuity remains higher than the HomeKeeper payout, but the disadvantage shrinks at higher levels of equity; thus, the former annuity would total $14,000 per year, versus $11,700 for the latter (only a 15% difference). This shrinking gap probably reflects the fact that the HomeKeeper loan is intended to attract homeowners with more valuable properties.

NOTES

1. Such problems might alter the terms of the RM policy, as suggested, for example, by Shiller and Weiss (1998), who propose that the loan be keyed not to the homeowner's own property appreciation but to a national housing index.
2. In the U.S. case, a white female population period mortality table (the decennial 1979–1981 life table) is used to price HECMs (Quercia, 1997). Using female instead of sex-specific cohort tables tends to make the loan amounts lower than they would be using male tables, whereas using population period tables rather than annuitant cohort tables would make the loan amounts higher than the alternative. It is not known whether RM borrowers have experienced actual mortality substantially different from projections. While Syzmanoski recognizes that HECM mortality might differ from population rates, he was unable to distinguish empirically between houses sold due to death versus termination for other reasons (Szymanoski and DiVenti, 2001). Lenders cannot take medical conditions into account when pricing RMs (Szymanoski, 1999), though Mayer and Simons (1994) suggest this might be a group likely to prefer RMs. In the latter case, underwriting could actually make the product more attractive for precisely those people who need it the most.
3. Fannie Mae provides homeowners with RM loans having higher limits than can be provided under the HECM program, namely $322,700 for 2003 (see www .reversemortgage.org/homekeep.htm).

Glossary

acceleration clause—the part of a contract that says when a loan may be declared due and payable.

adjustable rate—an interest rate that changes, based on changes in a published market-rate index.

appraisal—an estimate of how much a house would sell for if it were sold; also called its market value.

appreciation—an increase in a home's value.

Area Agency on Aging (AAA)—a local or regional nonprofit organization that provides information on services and programs for older adults.

cap—a limit on the amount an adjustable interest rate may go up or down during a specified time period.

closing—a meeting where documents are signed to "close the deal" on a mortgage; the time a mortgage begins.

CMT rate—the Constant Maturity Treasury rate, used as an interest rate index in the HECM program.

condemnation—a court action saying a property is unfit for use; also, the government taking private property to use for the public by the right of eminent domain.

creditline—a credit account that lets a borrower decide when to take money out and also how much to take out; also known as a "line-of-credit" or "credit line."

current interest rate—in the HECM program, the interest rate currently being charged on a loan, which equals one of the HUD-approved interest rate indices (1-month CMT, 1-year CMT, or 1-month LIBOR) plus a margin.

deferred payment loans (DPLs)—reverse mortgages that give you a lump sum of cash to repair or improve a home; usually offered by state or local governments.

depreciation—a decrease in the value of a home.

eminent domain—the right of a government to take private property for public use; for example, taking private land to build a highway.

expected interest rate—in the HECM program, the interest rate used to determine a borrower's loan advance amounts; equals either the 10-year CMT or the 10-year LIBOR rate plus a margin (see below).

Fannie Mae—a private company that buys and sells mortgages; a government-sponsored business that is watched over by the federal government.

Federal Housing Administration (FHA)—the part of the U.S. Department of Housing and Urban Development (HUD) that insures HECM loans.

federally insured reverse mortgage—a reverse mortgage guaranteed by the federal government so you will always get what the loan promises; also, a Home Equity Conversion Mortgage (HECM).

fixed monthly loan advances—payments of the same amount that are made to a borrower each month.

home equity—the value of a home, subtracting any money owed on it.

home equity conversion—turning home equity into cash without having to leave your home or make regular loan repayments.

Home Equity Conversion Mortgage (HECM)—the only reverse mortgage program insured by the Federal Housing Administration, a federal government agency.

home value limit—in the HECM program, the largest home value that can be used to determine a borrower's loan advances.

initial interest rate—in the HECM program, the interest rate that is first charged on the loan beginning at closing; equals one of the HUD-approved interest rate indices (1-month CMT, 1-year CMT, or 1-month LIBOR) plus a margin.

leftover equity—the sale price of the home minus the total amount owed on it and the cost of selling it; the amount the homeowner or heirs get when the house is sold.

LIBOR—the London Interbank Offered Rate, used as an interest rate index in the HECM program.

loan advances—payments made to a borrower, or to another party on behalf of a borrower.

loan balance—the amount owed, including principal and interest; capped in a reverse mortgage by the value of the home when the loan is repaid.

lump sum—a single loan advance at closing.

margin—in the HECM program, the amount added to an interest rate index to determine the initial, current, and expected interest rates.

maturity—when a loan must be repaid; when it becomes "due and payable."

model specifications—rules recommended by AARP for analyzing and comparing reverse mortgages.

mortgage—a legal document making a home available to a lender to repay a debt.

nonrecourse mortgage—a home loan in which the borrower generally cannot owe more than the home's value at the time the loan is repaid.

origination—the process of setting up a mortgage, including preparing documents.

property tax deferral (PTD)—reverse mortgages that pay annual property taxes; usually offered by state or local governments.

proprietary reverse mortgage—a reverse mortgage product owned by a private company.

reverse mortgage—a home loan that gives cash advances to a homeowner, requires no repayment until a future time, and is capped by the value of the home when the loan is repaid.

right of recission—a borrower's right to cancel a home loan within three business days of the closing.

securitization—the transformation of a pool of financial assets (e.g., mortgages) into securities (asset-backed securities).

servicing—administering a loan after closing, such as maintaining loan records and sending statements.

Supplemental Security Income (SSI)—a federal monthly income program for low-income persons who are aged 65+, blind, or disabled.

tenure advances—fixed monthly loan advances for as long as a borrower lives in a home.

term advances—fixed monthly loan advances for a specific period of time.

total annual loan cost (TALC) rate—the projected annual average cost of a reverse mortgage including all itemized costs.

About the Author

Vishaal B. Bhuyan has over five years of experience in the longevity and mortality risk markets. Vishaal has advised a number of large investment funds on life settlements, and more recently on reverse mortgages.

Mr. Bhuyan has been invited to speak at various life settlement and reverse mortgage conferences in addition to general hedge fund conferences across the United States, Europe, and Asia. He is the editor and co-author of *Life Markets: Trading Mortality and Longevity Risk with Life Settlements and Linked Securities* (2009, John Wiley & Sons) and author of *The Esoteric Investor* (2011, FT Press).

Vishaal has developed proprietary pricing and asset management technologies to create efficiency in the investing and trading of life settlements and has developed a streamlined origination process to generate high risk-adjusted returns for investors that addresses many of the risks present in the asset class.

Vishaal has been featured/quoted in, or contributed to: *Trader Monthly*, *Investment Dealers Digest*, *The Life Settlement Report*, *The Reverse Mortgage Report*, and *Roubini Global Economics Monitor*.

Vishaal graduated from the University of Pennsylvania in 2005 with a BA in the History and Sociology of Science.

About the Contributors

Micah Bloomfield has a broad-based practice, with a particular emphasis on financial products, including asset-backed securities transactions, life settlement transactions, and structured notes. He has considerable experience with tax issues that come up in bankruptcies or pre-bankruptcy workouts, and with hedge fund and other private equity funds.

Mr. Bloomfield also has advised dealers and other participants in numerous swap and other derivatives transactions. In connection with cross-border swap transactions, he drafted model tax modules that can be used for negotiating ISDA tax representations and related tax forms. He is an active member of ISDA's tax committee. Recent projects include:

- Co-authoring a revision of *Real Estate Investment Trusts* (Securities Law Series).
- Helping formulate a Special Report of the New York State Bar Association on the taxation of life settlements.
- Commenting on legislation that would provide voluntary tax assessments to fund loans to retrofit buildings with renewable-energy and energy-saving devices.

Michael V. Fasano is president and CEO of Fasano Associates, a leading underwriting consulting firm providing life expectancy estimates to the life settlement industry. He has served on the Board of the Life Insurance Settlement Association (LISA) for the past four years, where he served on the Membership Committee and chaired LISA's Task Force developing best practice standards for life expectancy providers. He also is a member of the Life Settlement Institute (LSI), the Institutional Life Markets Association (ILMA), and the German Life Settlement Association, BVZL. He was named one of the most influential people in the life settlement industry by *Life Settlement Review*. He is a frequent industry speaker and has published articles in *Best's Review*, *Pensions and Investments*, and the *National Underwriter*.

Before starting Fasano Associates, Mr. Fasano served as president of Trans-General Life Insurance Company; and before that, he worked at the White House Office of Management and Budget.

Mr. Fasano received his BA from Northwestern University and his MA from the University of Wisconsin, Madison. He currently serves on the Board of Visitors for Northwestern University's College of Arts & Sciences.

Kai Gilkes, Victoria Johnstone, Apea Koranteng, Karen Naylor, and **Andrea Quirk** are analysts with Standard & Poor's.

Standard & Poor's: With offices in 23 countries and a history that dates back 150 years, Standard & Poor's (S&P) is known to investors worldwide as a leader in financial-market intelligence. Today, Standard & Poor's strives to provide investors who want to make better-informed investment decisions with market intelligence in the form of credit ratings, indices, investment research, and risk evaluations and solutions.

Most notably, Standard & Poor's is known as an independent provider of credit ratings. In 2008, it published more than one million new and revised credits ratings and rated more than US$32 trillion in outstanding debt. Standard & Poor's is also widely known for maintaining one of the most widely followed indices of large-cap American stocks: the S&P 500. In 2007, the S&P 500 celebrated its fiftieth anniversary.

Additionally, the S&P Global 1200 covers approximately 30 markets constituting approximately 70 percent of global market capitalization. Currently, there are more than $1.5 trillion in investment assets directly tied to S&P indices and approximately $5 trillion is benchmarked to S&P indices—more than all other index providers combined.

Moreover, Standard & Poor's independent equity research business is among the world's leading providers of independent investment information, offering fundamental coverage on approximately 2,000 stocks. S&P is also a leader in mutual fund information and analysis.

Peter Macrae Mazonas, CPA, is a managing member at Life Settlement Financial, LLC. He founded Life Settlement Financial (LSF) in 2006 to offer transparency and efficiency as both a life settlement provider and capital markets company serving the life settlement marketplace. At the core are principles consistent with generally accepted auditing and asset valuation techniques. Life Settlement Financial owns the commercial rights to Longevity Cost Calculator™ (LCC), originally peer reviewed and published in the *North American Actuarial Journal*. This health and degradation of health life expectancy assessment model has 96 percent actual to expected chi-square and linear regression validated accuracy.

Mr. Mazonas has a broad background in finance, accounting, corporate governance, business asset valuation, and computer modeling.

He started his business career at Price Waterhouse & Co. Before founding LSF, Mazonas acted as interim COO/CFO of Archimedes Inc., an evidence-based quantitative pharmaco/economic model for predictive analysis of new drugs and patient therapies for big pharma, national therapy advocacy associations, and large Fortune 500 companies. He was director of Corporate Governance and Sarbanes Oxley compliance for the $90 billion McKesson Corp. and a co-founder, president, and CEO of Transamerica HomeFirst, a market leader reverse mortgage lender. Mr. Mazonas created the first patented lifetime reverse mortgage products and developed the methods to securitize reverse mortgages as the first longevity-valued asset class. He created and managed the Executive Financial Counseling (EFC) and later Private Banking Division at Bank of America, which specialized in financial planning, wealth management, and credit and transaction structuring for senior corporate executives and affluent families.

Olivia S. Mitchell is International Foundation of Employee Benefit Plans Professor of Insurance and Risk Management; executive director of the Pension Research Council; and director of the Boettner Center on Pensions and Retirement Research, all at the Wharton School of the University of Pennsylvania. She is also a research associate at the National Bureau of Economic Research and a co-investigator for the Health and Retirement Study at the University of Michigan. Her research focuses on private and public insurance, risk management, public finance, and compensation and pensions, and her work on Social Security reform won TIAA-CREF's Paul Samuelson Award for "Outstanding Writing on Lifelong Financial Security." She also received the Premio Internazionale Dell'Istituto Nazionale Delle Assicurazioni (INA) from the Accademia Nazionale dei Lincei, Rome, Italy ex aqueo; the 2007 Fidelity Institute Research Prize; and the 2008 Roger F. Murray First Prize from the Institute for Quantitative Research in Finance. She previously taught at Cornell University, Harvard University, the Goethe University of Frankfurt, Singapore Management University, and the University of New South Wales. She served on the Commission to Strengthen Social Security, the U.S. Department of Labor's ERISA Advisory Council, and the Advisory Committee of the Central Provident Fund Board of Singapore. She received her BA in Economics from Harvard University and MA and PhD degrees in Economics from the University of Wisconsin, Madison. See also www.wharton.upenn.edu/faculty/mitchelo.html.

Nemo Perera and **Chris DeSilva** are managing partners at Risk Capital Partners.

Risk Capital Partners: With offices in New York, Philadelphia, and Los Angeles, Risk Capital Partners (RCP) is a boutique insurance consultancy and brokerage that specializes in modeling actuarial data, developing complex underwriting pitch books, and drafting sample policies for clients who seek to mitigate unconventional risks in the insurance and capital markets. We are unique due to: our exclusive focus on the mitigation and placement of complex risks; our proven track record developing unique risk transfer products that enable complex transactions; our extensive network of senior-level contacts among property and casualty carriers, life carriers, reinsurers, and financial markets; our continuous efforts to research and develop new risk transfer vehicles to unlock hidden financial value; our unparalleled risk finance knowledge, skills, and credibility with insurers; our integrity; and our commitment as a boutique firm to serve our clients to the best of our abilities.

John Piggott has served as Professor of Economics at the University of New South Wales since 1988. He holds a BA from the University of Sydney, and MSc and PhD degrees from the University of London. He is also director of the university's newly established Australian Institute of Population Ageing Research. Past appointments include research and teaching positions at the University of Western Ontario, Canada, and at the Australian National University, Canberra. He was elected a Fellow of the Academy of the Social Sciences in Australia in 1992.

Professor Piggott has a longstanding interest in issues relating to retirement and pension economics and finance. His publications include more than 80 journal articles and chapters in books, which have appeared in the leading international academic journals as well as in highly cited conference volumes. In addition, he has co-authored two books, both published by Cambridge University Press. The second of these, on mandatory pension saving, was released in late 2001.

For some years now, he has had a policy and research interest in the evolving pension reform debate in the Asian region. For the past several years, he has been working on aging issues with the Cabinet Office, Government of Japan, and he recently concluded an evaluation of World Bank assistance on pension reform in the Asian region for the Bank's Operations Evaluation Department. He was earlier involved in a major project on annuity design for the funded portion of Russia's pension system. Current external appointments include membership on the Governing Board of the Indian Pension Research Foundation and scientific advisor to the Frisch Center for Economic Research, University of Oslo. He is on the editorial board of the new Cambridge journal, the *Journal of Pension Economics and Finance*.

Professor Piggott's university administration includes two periods as head of the School of Economics (1988–1989 and 1997–2002), two terms as the Faculty's Presiding Member (1992–1997), and more than six years as its Associate Dean of Research (2002–2009). He has also served as a director of the UNSW Professorial Superannuation Scheme (1998–2003).

Joseph Selvidio focuses his practice on the convergence of capital markets and insurance, traditional and esoteric structured finance transactions, and alternative energy financings. He has represented investment banks, hedge funds, and other institutional investors in structuring insurance-linked securitizations with an emphasis on life settlements and premium finance and other longevity/mortality–related transactions.

Since February 2009, Mr. Selvidio has represented leading investment banks such as Citigroup Global Markets Inc. as underwriter's counsel in both public and private student loan securitizations in excess of $5 billion. He is also actively involved in the representation of the Institutional Life Markets Association Inc., a not-for-profit trade association formed to educate consumers, investors, and policymakers about the benefits of the mortality- and longevity-related marketplace.

Representative Matters in the Longevity and Mortality Marketplace:

- Represented European investment bank in structuring the purchase of 100 percent participation interests in life insurance premium finance loans originated by a U.S. lending company.
- Represented a variety of lenders in developing and administering life insurance premium finance lending programs.
- Advised in the development of an investment fund formed to purchase life settlements and structured settlements.
- Worked with policymakers in a variety of states in drafting life settlement laws and regulations.

Charles Stone is an associate professor at Brooklyn College, CUNY. He teaches Investments and Corporate Finance. As a member of the consortial faculty of CUNY's School of Professional Studies since 2007, Charles worked with his colleagues to develop and launch online BS and MS programs in business. Charles earned his PhD in economics from the CUNY Graduate Center. He is a leading expert in asset-backed securities and senior life settlements securitization, has edited several books on the subject, and recently co-authored with Anne Zissu *The Securitization Markets Handbook: Issuing and Investing in Mortgage- and Asset-Backed Securities*, Bloomberg Press, 2005. His research has appeared in leading academic journals, including the *Journal of Real Estate, Finance and Economics*, the *FNMA Journal of Housing Research*, the *Journal of Derivatives*, the *Journal of Applied Corporate Finance*, the *Journal of Risk Finance*, the *Journal of Alternative Investments*, and *Financial Markets, Institutions and Instruments*. He has been an expert witness in several cases of securitization transactions. Professor Stone has been invited to lecture on Securitization at several institutions, such as the ISMA Centre, Reading University, in England; Paris-Dauphine University, in Paris; Ecole Superieure de Commerce de Paris; the Inter-American Development Bank, in Washington, D.C.; the

Securities and Exchange Commission, in Washington D.C.; J. P. Morgan in New York; Bear Stearns in New York; ESSEC in Paris; HEC, Paris; the Fletcher School of Law and Diplomacy at Tufts University; Euromoney, in New York; Euromoney in Paris; Euromoney in London; NYU-Poly, in the Master of Financial Engineering. He is currently analyzing the crash of the subprime mortgage market and the resulting contagion.

Boris Ziser has more than 10 years of experience across diverse asset classes. He focuses on public and private mortgage-backed and asset-backed securitizations, warehouse facilities, commercial paper conduits, and related transactions. Mr. Ziser's practice encompasses commercial mortgage-backed transactions, as well as a variety of asset classes such as life settlements, equipment leases, structured settlements, auto loans, and franchise loans, in addition to esoteric asset classes such as timeshare loans and intellectual property. He counsels issuers, investors, lenders, borrowers, underwriters, and placement agents on a variety of matters. Mr. Ziser is fluent in Russian.

Mr. Ziser is also one of the leading attorneys in the life settlement industry. He represents investors, lenders, hedge funds, and providers in a wide range of transactions, including purchase platforms, lending platforms, fund formation, warehouse facilities, and commercial paper conduit transactions. He is listed in *Chambers USA*.

While at Stroock or prior to joining the firm in 2007, Mr. Ziser's experience has included:

- Representing clients in establishing multiple life settlement and premium finance funds.
- Representing clients in establishing life insurance premium finance platforms.
- Representing clients in U.S. and offshore life settlement transactions.
- Issuers' and underwriters' counsel in connection with numerous commercial mortgage and asset-backed securitization transactions.
- Securitization of commercial mortgage B-Notes.
- Timeshare receivables warehouse facilities and securitization transactions.

Anne Zissu is chair of the Department of Business at Citytech, City University of New York and a research fellow at the Polytechnic Institute of NYU. She is the co-founding editor of *The Financier*, and *The Securitization Conduit*, publications providing analysis on corporate finance, risk management, securitization, and related topics. She is a leading expert in asset-backed securities and senior life settlements securitization, has edited several books on the subject, and recently completed *The Securitization*

Markets Handbook: Issuing and Investing in Mortgage- and Asset-Backed Securities, Bloomberg Press, 2005. Her research has appeared in leading academic journals, including the *Journal of Real Estate, Finance and Economics*, the *FNMA Journal of Housing Research*, the *Journal of Derivatives*, the *Journal of Applied Corporate Finance*, the *Journal of Risk Finance*, the *Journal of Alternative Investments*, and *Financial Markets, Institutions and Instruments*. She has been an expert witness in several cases of securitization transactions. Professor Zissu (Professor at Temple University from 1988 to 2008) has been invited to lecture on Securitization at several institutions such as the ISMA Centre, Reading University, in England; Paris-Dauphine University, in Paris; Ecole Superieure de Commerce de Paris; the Inter-American Development Bank, in Washington, D.C.; the Securities and Exchange Commission, in Washington D.C.; J. P. Morgan in New York; Bear Stearns in New York; ESSEC in Paris; the Fletcher School of Law and Diplomacy at Tufts University; Euromoney, in New York; Euromoney, in Paris; Euromoney, in London; NYU-Poly, in the Master of Financial Engineering.

Index